Phoenix Rising

Phoenix Rising
The Next Generation of American Formal Poets

Edited by Sonny Williams

Textos Books

Published by Textos Books
P.O. Box 541106
Cincinnati, OH 45254-1106

ISBN: 1932339450
LCCN: 2004100573

Poetry Editor: Kevin Walzer
Business Editor: Lori Jareo

Typeset in Transitional 511 by WordTech Communications LLC, Cincinnati, OH

Visit us on the web at www.textos-books.com

Cover art courtesy David Bates, Dunn and Brown Contemporary, and The Art Museum of Southeast Texas.

Contents

Acknowledgments

I am grateful to the authors, editors, and publishers who have given me permission to reprint the poems.

Craig Arnold, "Tune into this," "The rain lets its fingers lift," "All I wanted were the flowers," first published in *Quarterly West*, "We are so practiced in the art," first published in *Euphony*, "Another April," first published in *Colorado Review*, appear by permission of the author.

Chris Baker, "Anniversary," first published in *Edge City Review*, "This Week in Verse," first published in *Light*, "One Last Request," "Jeremy Jerrell," "A Prostitute's Reply to a Pimp," appear by permission of the author.

Bill Coyle, "The Magic Circle," first published in *The Hudson Review*, "Leave Taking" and "Perspectives," first published in *Dark Horse*, "The Flautist of North Station," first published in *The Formalist*, appear by permission of the author.

Jill Alexander Essbaum, "Wednesday, Ash" and "Concerning the End of Us," reprinted from *Heaven* (University Press of New England, 2000), "Death Song," "Hotel Infinity," "Cemetery Road," "Despair," "Fissure," appear by permission of the author.

Jenny Factor, "Song from a Sippy Cup," first published in *The Beloit Poetry Journal*, "Summer Journal, Israel (Age 19)," "Extramarital...," "Happenstance," "Réunion À Deux," "While Undressing...," "Riqueza," reprinted from *Unraveling at the Name* (Copper Canyon Press, 2002), appear by permission of the author.

Ted Genoways, "Outside the Slaughterhouse," "The Killing Floor," reprinted from *Bullroarer: A Sequence* (Northeastern University Press, 2001), "Letters from Eagle," first published in *American Literary Review*, "After an Unframed Original," first published in *Southern Review*, "The Slaughterhouse Wall," first published in *Partisan Review*, appear by permission of the author.

Beth Gylys, "The Trouble with Love Poems about Men," "Marriage Song," "Preference," "Desire," reprinted from *Bodies that Hum* (Silverfish Review

Press, 1999), appear by permission of the author.

Adam Kirsch, "Balsam," "Heroes Have the Whole Earth for Their Tomb," "Three Odes after Horace," reprinted from *The Thousand Wells* (Ivan R. Dee, 2002), "Classic Crimes," "The long, squat, leaden-windowed, burrow-like," "Calmly, the papers calculate the chance," appear by permission of the author.

April Lindner, "Girl," "Crystal," "The Rubin Vase," reprinted from *Skin* (Texas Tech University Press, 2002), appear by permission of the author.

Joshua Mehigan, "The Optimist," first published in *Poetry*, "Confusing Weather," first published in *Ploughshares*, "The Tyrant," first published in *The Formalist*, "The Murder," first published in *Orbis*, "War Dims Hopes for Peace," first published in *Parnassus: Poetry in Review*, appear by permission of the author.

Joe Osterhaus, "Dayr Amis," "Lake Endeavor," "Running of the Blues," reprinted from *Radiance* (Zoo Press, 2002), appear by permission of the author.

Alison Pelegrin, "I'm Gonna Leave You, Chère," "The Summer of *The Joy of Sex*," "Bordelon's Blues," "The Fiddle Player to His Love," "Eunice Plays the Field: A Trenta-Sei," "The Zydeco Tablet," reprinted from *The Zydeco Tablets* (Word Press, 2002), appear by permission of the author.

V. Penelope Pelizzon, "Hours," "Songs for the Boisterous Month," first published in the *Southeast Review*, "Acqua Alta," first published in *Web Del Sol*, appear by permission of the author.

Chelsea Rathburn, "Argument in a Restaurant," "Sixteen," first published in *The Formalist*, "Unused Lines," first published in *The New Criterion*, "Fireworks," "Eurydice Alive," appear by permission of the author.

Jennifer Reeser, "The Centerfold," first published in *Pivot*, "Not Even in Dreams," first published in *The Lyric*, "An Envelope for Jason," first published in *The Neovictorian/Cochlea*, "Why It Wasn't You," first published in *The Alsop Review*, "When I am Dead my Dearest...," first published in *The Louisiana Review*, appear by permission of the author. Poems also appeared in *An Alabaster Flask* (Word Press, 2003.)

A. E. Stallings, "Explaining an Affinity for Bats," first published in *The Formalist*, "The Charioteer," first published in the *Sewanee Theological Review*, "Implements from the 'Tomb of the Poet,'""Arrowhead Hunting," first published in *Poetry*, "An Ancient Dog Grave, Unearthed During Construction of the Athens Metro," first published in *The Hudson Review*, "Thyme," first published in *Shenandoah*, appear by permission of the author.

Philip Stephens, "God Shed His Grace," "Vineyard," "Hangman," "Ditch Digging," reprinted from *The Determined Days* (The Overlook Press, 2000), "Everyman's Actor," first published in the *Oxford American*, "Nativity," first published in the *Kansas City Star*, appear by permission of the author.

Diane Thiel, "Love Letters," "Memento Mori in Middle School," "Bedside Readers," "At the Mailbox," "Echolocations," reprinted from *Echolocations* (Story Line Press, 2000), "Editorial Suggestive," first published in *Dark Horse*, "Daphne," first published in *Rattapallax*, appear by permission of the author.

Jennifer Tonge, "Invitation," first published in the *New England Review*, "Tankas for Roxi," first published in the *Cream City Review*, "Acrostic at Sarah's Request," first published in *Ploughshares*, "The Mudanya Fig," "The Turkish Pear," first published in *The Madison Review*, "Peach," first published in *Poetry*, "The Bursa Peach," appear by permission of the author.

Catherine Tufariello, "The Walrus at Coney Island," "Elegy for Alice," reprinted from *Free Time* (R. L. Barth, 2001), "No Angel," "Rebekah," reprinted from *Annunciations* (Aralia Press, 2001), "Useful Advice," first published in *Tar River Poetry*, "The Feast of the Tabernacles," "Fruitless," first published in *Poetry*, appear by permission of the author.

Kevin Walzer, "The Touch of Marriage," "A Subjunctive Divorce," "Underwork," "Before His Healing," reprinted from *Greater Circles* (Word Press, 2001), appear by permission of the author.

Rachel Wetzsteon, "Love and Work," first published in *The New Yorker*, "Little Song for a Big Night," first published in *Salmagundi*, "Madeline for Awhile," first published in *The Threepenny Review*, "Homage to Eddie Izzard," first published in *The Paris Review*, appear by permission of the author.

Sonny Williams, "The Playboy," "The Ballad of the Search Party," first published in *Pivot*, "Playing Basketball," first published in *Word Journal*, "Death in Dallas," appear by permission of the author.

Greg Williamson, "Origami," "Double Exposures," "The Muse Addresses the Poet (and getteth alle up in hys face)," "The Life and Times of Wile E. Coyote, Super Genius," reprinted from *Errors in the Script* (The Overlook Press, 2001), appear by permission of the author.

Christian Wiman, "A Field in Scurry County" and "Sleeping in the Open," first published in the *New Criterion*, "Rhymes for a Watertower," first published in *Slate*, "Poŝtolka," first published in *The Atlantic Monthly*, "Hard Night," first published in the *New England Review*, "Old Song, Long Night," appear by permission of the author.

Chryss Yost, "Terzanelle in Blonde," "Lai with Sound of Skin," "Advice for Women," reprinted from *La Jolla Boys* (Mille Grazie Press, 2000), appear by permission of the author.

Michael T. Young, "The Fall in Voter Turnout," first published in *Pivot*, "Letter from a Baychester Resident," "Surfaces," appear by permission of the author.

Preface

I
"Our generation has an important voice, but no one seems to hear it."
Ted Halstead, President of the New American Foundation, "A Politics for Generation X," *The Atlantic Online*, August 1999

We have been called the 13th generation, the "grunge" generation, and the new "lost" generation. We are the products of dysfunctional families, video games, and MTV. We have been much maligned, commercialized, and media-stuffed. However, this generation, popularly known as Gen X, has yet to be properly represented for its poetry. Being a Gen Xer and a poet-critic, I have frequently been asked who the younger poets are, what are their subjects, and in what forms are they writing. To answer these questions, I have chosen twenty-seven poets, all born between 1960 and 1976, and each poet has provided a brief statement on the forms they use and why. My objective has been to provide a forum in which the voices of this generation that few have heard could be presented.

Who or what, then, is Generation X? Does the term really mean anything? Much of how people perceive Generation X was expressed in several forms and generally began in 1991. Some of the more popular representations of Gen X are the movie *Slacker*, directed by Richard Linklater; Douglas Copeland's book *Generation X: Tales for an Accelerated Culture*; and the rise of rap and grunge music. This was the birth of Generation X, of living life without direction. Our predecessors, that demographic bulge known as the Baby Boomers, have labeled us crybabies who need to grow up. We have been stereotyped as slackers, losers, whiners, cynics, drifters, malcontents, and apathetic. As with most stereotypes, there are some truths but many more inaccuracies. How does one sum up the character of a whole generation? What, if any, are the common experiences between individuals born a decade or more apart? Do not ethnicity, social class, geography, temperament, individual experience, and ideology provide us with better distinctions than one that is generational? Though finding any certain shared assumptions and experiences or a common aesthetic among all of the poets of this generation would be largely untenable, I will speculate that some commonalities do exist, some shared cultural affinities, that transcend the polarizing forces of racial and socioeconomic identity.

Much has been written about this generation and much more thoroughly than I am able to do here, but some of the more shared assumptions of this group follow. William Strauss and Neil Howe, in their essay "The New Generation Gap," define this generation as those born between 1961-1981. We are a disengaged generation who would rather play than work. Unlike our parents who were optimistic and seemed to get richer, our economic future is uncertain, though we are increasingly materialistic. Our view of the American Dream is a bleak one, as we see ourselves having to bear much of the burden as the Boomers age (These aging millions will want their entitlements, and who will have to support them?). We tried to discover what to do with our lives and are still unsure of the future. We took longer to leave the house and put off major decisions such as marriage and careers. Seeing our jobs as just a way to get money, we live paycheck to paycheck, spending impulsively and fitting the "slacker" stereotype. We do not have the dreamy, idealistic, go-getter attitude that our parents had. We are oblivious to the larger world around us and to the news media. We are not revolutionaries because, as we often say, what would be the point?

Indeed, few of us are politically involved or have hopes that we can affect any kind of change. Ted Halstead, in his article "A Politics for Generation X," states, "A wide sampling of surveys indicates that Xers are less politically or civically engaged, exhibit less social trust or confidence in government, have a weaker allegiance to their country or to either political party, and are more materialistic than their predecessors." We have no faith in our future. Instead, we are looking for an anaesthetic to ease the pain, not a cure for the disease. Unlike the optimistic, placard-carrying, change-the-world attitude of our parents, we simply do not care. Strauss and Howe reveal this counter-mood; "It's a tone of physical frenzy and spiritual numbness, a revelry of pop, a pursuit of high-tech, guiltless fun. It's a carnival culture featuring the tangible bottom lines of life—money, bodies, and brains—and the wordless deals with which one can be traded for another. A generation weaned on minimal expectations and gifted in the game of life is now avoiding meaning in a cumbersome society that, as they see it, offers them little." We have no confidence in institutions, whether they are economic, educational, business, or religious. Farai Chideya, a Gen Xer and ABC News correspondent, suggests that young Americans are not just bored but are disenfranchised from the political system. Halstead agrees by saying we have been duped and ignored by it.

But we are also a lucky generation. We inherited the victories of the Civil Rights and Women's Movements. We have not experienced a national crisis or a hot war, though the fear of nuclear annihilation was never far from our minds. The closest thing we experienced to a war growing up was the 1991 Persian Gulf conflict, but the war was televised and it was brief, perfectly fitting our experiences and expectations. For us the war was like a video game. Those who fought in World War II saw that conflict as a heroic fight against a great evil. The Boomers had Vietnam, a war that pitted generations against each other. The Xers had cartoons and Space Invaders. Unlike preceding generations, there was no seminal event to which we could all respond. We have grown up in a very different world of television, cable, remote controls, interactive games and computers. In opposition to Halstead and Chideya, Tucker Carlson of *The Weekly Standard*, who was born in 1969, believes it is our country's very prosperity and tranquility that makes it so we do not have to be informed or actively engaged. "Generation X is in debt precisely because it *isn't* worried about the future...And that's also why it doesn't vote."

For Boomers, we represent America in decline. We are driven by appetites, those of pleasure and pain, rather than cerebral or spiritual pursuits. We see no conflict between personal wealth and liberty. We have a short attention span. We do not follow the workaholic, value-fixed lifestyle of the Boomers. Instead, as Strauss and Howe reveal, "Like warriors on the eve of battle, Thirteeners face their future with a mixture of bravado and fatalism. Squared off competitively against one another, this melange of scared city kids, suburban slackers, hungry immigrants, desperate grads, and shameless hustlers is collectively coming to realize that America rewards only a select set of winners with its Dream—and that America cares little about its anonymous losers."

Not all descriptions are doom and gloom. We're hardworking, resourceful, pragmatic, multi-taskers who can process information quickly. We embrace change. We are flexible and adaptable. We have rejected the neopuritanism and sermonizing of our predecessors. Instead, we are tolerant to different sexual, social, and religious mores. For us, the future is uncertain, so we have a carpe diem attitude. We want to enjoy the moment. Our diffidence is an aspect of our intelligence, for we are careful not to commit to anything for fear of getting burned. However, to this day, Generation Xers have not rebutted the Boomer assessment of them. We are withdrawn, characterized by ironic detachment, perhaps as a coping mechanism for a world increasingly overloaded with information. When we are faced with the self-righteous preaching of our elders, our strategy has been blatantly non-confrontational as we frequently respond with "Whatever." Such apathetic responses have been often viewed as part of the moral blight or youthful stupidity that plagues America's future.

Halstead suggests that this generation needs to have a collective politics, a collective voice that will spur change. However, we are not burgeoning revolutionaries. We view political parties, Republican and Democratic alike, as corrupt, having experienced first hand the political scandals from Nixon to Clinton. The old Left-Right model of political correctness versus moral correctness simply isn't working. Yet, Scott Stossel, editor of *The American Prospect*, does not see such collective politics re-engaging our contemporaries in public life. Chideya agrees: "Creating a third (and fourth and fifth) viable political party would revolutionize and energize the political process, but it is hard to envision such a change given our laws and the informal structures of political financing that support the Republican and Democratic parties."

Though I do not think it possible, or desirable, to have generational political solidarity, we do tend to recognize the valid ideals of both the Left and Right. If there is something that may bind all of us, it is the near-universal Gen-X desire for greater individual choice, greater economic fairness, and greater global connectedness. The tragic events of 9/11 and the War on Terror that followed also connect us. How will we deal with foreign policy and home security in the future? At the very least, the poets in this anthology are connected by their love of poetry, language, and artful expression of human experience. It is their very open-mindedness, yet concern with craft, that allows for rich and engaging poetry. It is poetry and the telling of stories that make our lives worthwhile. This active participation in the arts is one way that our voices may be heard, and, perhaps, it is through poetry that Gen Xers may be galvanized.

II

"If it should happen that the men of some period were agreed upon any such rules, that would prove nothing for the following period; for among democratic nations each new generation is a new people. Among such nations, then, literature will not easily be subjected to strict rules, and it is impossible that any such rules should ever be permanent."

> Alexis de Tocqueville, *Democracy in America*, Chapter XIII, Volume II, 1840

In an interview with J. D. McClatchy, which appeared in "The Art of Poetry XXXX: Anthony Hecht," *Paris Review* 30 (fall 1988), Hecht states, "I prefer the work that is decidedly more architectural, in which parts balance one another, and in which everything is essential, so that if something is removed or misplaced, the whole thing collapses." Though not new, the architectural metaphor is an appropriate one. The vocabulary of architecture, such as form and structure, is very similar to that of poetry. Regardless of the forms an architect may use, the structure must still stand. Such is true for poetry. The question is how far can a poem be pushed structurally before it falls apart? When discussing poetry, the concept of form is hotly debated, and poets are quick to plant flags in divisive, hostile camps.

Michael Schmidt in *Lives of the Poets* states, "what matters as poetry is form." No good poem is formless. Poets must use some kind of language system, whether metered or unmetered. All such systems are "formal" in that they provide a means of shaping and unifying. Such a view allows a more varied and challenging approach to form. If one abandons syllabic and accentual regularity, then one must create linguistic patterning in some other way by using lineation, enjambement, stanzas, rhymes, parallel structuring, rhythmic patterning or pacing of syntax. Many poets and critics have wrestled with the different notions about form, specifically the relationship between formal verse and free verse. Certainly, the old division of "formal" verse and "free" verse is simplistic and inappropriate. The terms "closed" and "open" also carry connotations that are misleading. Amy Lowell calls free verse "polyphonic prose." Donald Davie prefers "unmetered verse." Lewis Turco thinks free verse to be a contradiction in terms and prefers "prose prosodies." Annie Finch has termed the many formal poetic traditions, including experimental traditions, as "multiformalism." Though the term multiformalism is encompassing, it smacks too much of the over-politicized term multiculturalism, and "formalism" itself, as Anne Stevenson puts it, "feels like fug." Yet, Finch is correct in her attempt to broaden the spectrum. Schmidt, too, "acknowledges diversity with commonality of resources." His approach to poetic form proposes "stable points of departure, even as it exemplifies difference and identifies the new." Each of the poets in this anthology approach form in much the same way. Meter and the tradition of English poetry acts as the touchstone from which these poets explore the new. Form can easily slip into format when the poet merely stuffs experience into a preconceived pattern. Seamus Heaney says, "I would make a distinction between form which is an act of living principle, and shape which is discernible on the page, but inaudible, and kinetically, muscularly, unavailable. Poetry is a muscular response." Form is more than simply counting syllables on fingers. My preference is for a poetry that is more audible rather than typographical. The poets in this anthology are audible (even as some experiment with typography), and they refer and respond to the forms and subjects that are available, not only in the English tradition, but from the literary traditions of various cultures around the world. In the process, we are able to use traditional forms as well as design our own patterns and forms, creating interesting compositions and structures that reflect our own varied experiences and preferences.

Unlike many of our predecessors, we do not believe that the structures and forms with which we choose to write align us politically with any particular school of thought, nor do we aspire to make some polemical statement. In fact, through the conversations I have had with the poets included, they are only vaguely aware of such contemporary movements as Expansive and Language poetry, and those who are more familiar with them have no desire to engage in the poetry wars. They feel no real connection to these movements, yet they have no antipathy for them either. Most find such labels as Expansive, Language, and Gen X confusing and confining. Instead, as the short discussions on form that each poet provided will reveal, these poets go with whatever works for them individually. We more or less follow the motto of "Just Do It." We are not dogmatic, nor are we dictatorial. However, this should not be misinterpreted as weak thinking or timidity. Rather, each poet works within rules applicable to his or her own writing, thereby allowing much more varied and interesting poetry. While talking with these poets, they reminded me of what Whitman said in his Preface to *Leaves of Grass*; "Whatever satisfies the soul is truth."

Just as Halstead believes that a new politics is necessary for this generation, so, too, would I suggest that the poetry of Gen X require a need for a different politics. One of the mistakes of many contemporary poets and critics is to assign the labels of conservative or liberal to poems based solely on their form. Is an anti-war poem conservative for being written as a sonnet? Is the frank expression of sexuality from a female perspective likewise conservative for being written in villanelles? Is someone who writes free verse automatically to be presumed a liberal, though free verse, which has so dominated the world of poetry for most of the twentieth century, has now become quite de rigueur? Certainly not. Whatever their political tastes, these poets reveal a wide range of approaches, styles, and subjects that cannot and should not be pigeonholed. They are not limited by current fashion or by rules of the past.

Much of this is possible because of the change in the editorial climate for poems written in traditional forms. During the sixties and seventies, the short, free verse lyric dominated, and these poems were usually autobiographical. The poets who started the Expansive movement over twenty years ago did much to invigorate form and storytelling in poetry. They provided alternative forms and styles to the free verse lyric, and they created outlets for these poems. Today, mainstream journals are publishing sonnets alongside free verse.

While the older generation wrote about the Vietnam War and the Beach Boys, we write about Wile E. Coyote and sex. There are poems about death, loss, and God. There are poems that are funny, satirical, robust, and self-effacing, while others are more soft-spoken and meditative. Some poems are written in strict iambic pentameters, while others are patterned more loosely. The most compelling similarity is the dramatic tenor of these poems, an audible, kinetic, and muscular poetry. What differentiates our poems from our elders' is the shoot-from-the-hip attitude that pervades them. We have no difficulty mixing popular and high culture. We're colloquial, slangy and playful and are inclined to sing. We love to tell stories, for we feel the need to develop our own identities and meanings.

A common point of discussion in each of the poet's statement is how form provides variety and music. Kevin Walzer says the "different fixed forms, such as the villanelle and the sonnet, offered yet further variety." Diane Thiel is "drawn to the possibilities of form" and its "musical possibilities." Ted Genoways believes writing in form makes his poetry "denser and richer." Another common point is the pleasure each poet derives from writing in form. Greg Williamson "likes the sport of it." Catherine Tufariello likes "the sheer pleasure that the pulse of meter and sounds of rhyme afford." Alicia Stallings feels it "brings pleasure to the reader and the writer." As can be seen, it is not political agenda or fashion that influences these poets. Rather, they write whatever pleases them and with whatever vehicles that can transport their experiences.

This generation is coming of age and can no longer be classified as McJobbers and wandering nomads of temporary employment. Many of these poets are taking important positions in the literary community and are beginning to be recognized for their talents. Christian Wiman has recently been appointed poetry editor of *Poetry*, a distinguished publication of verse. Adam Kirsch is a book critic at the *New York Sun* and writes criticism for several publications. Kevin Walzer has daringly begun his own literary journal, *Word Journal*, and press, Word Press. Some are teachers in university creative writing departments. Some are Fulbright Scholars, and some have been awarded NEA fellowships. Many have recently won a number of poetry awards such as the Yale Series of Younger Poets, the Bakeless Prize, the Hayden Carruth Award, and the Nicholas Roerich Prize. A few have already published several books, while others have yet to do so. I am proud to say that many of the poems included here have only been published in literary journals, and some are making their first appearance. It is much safer to include poets and poems that have already gone through the editorial mill. My hope has been to present new voices and fresh poems. Whatever each poet's politics may be, ultimately, the poems speak for themselves.

* * *

Endeavors of this sort are rarely the result of one individual. I would like to thank all of the contributors for their generosity, participation, and timely responses. Many took the time to negotiate with publishers to make permission fees manageable. I would especially like to thank Chris Baker, Ted Genoways, Alicia Stallings, Catherine Tufariello, and Christian Wiman for their helpful comments and recommendations. Also, I would like to thank those dreaded Boomers, Dana Gioia and Frederick Turner, for their kind suggestions. Mostly, I would like to thank Kevin Walzer and Lori Jareo for their dedication in taking on this project. This book exists because of them. It is the energy and imagination of individuals such as these who will give our generation a voice. Finally, I am grateful to my patient wife, Loreé, my favorite Gen Xer.

Craig Arnold (1967)

After Thomas Carlye, tailor retailored & premodern postmodernist:

If style is the dress of thought, then the New Formalism was Casual Friday, with its khakis and loafers and pastel Oxford with the top button open, the carefully affected disarray of a coat and tie just removed, Hi, My Name is Brad, Hi, My Name is Dana, and its three-ring binder of corporate cultural literacy, sonnet, villanelle or sestina; it didn't matter what rules were followed as long as they were rules, and someone else's. Of course it's no fun to play tennis without a net, but tennis is not the only game, white is not my favorite color, it's such a bitch to keep clean, and anyway they don't let the likes of us into the country club except maybe through the back door.

Tcha.

But consider form, also, as dress-up, form as drag, form as glam, form as bling-bling, form as vintage thrift, form as vestments, form as the uniform of your favorite Village Person, form as Holly Golightly's lipstick-kissed elbow gloves, form as the sense of flair and fabulousness that is the natural inheritance of anyone with a good eye and a bad ass, form as the consolation of those who miss the dandies of some other era, doubtless imaginary, who knew how to dress up and what for, dinner, dancing, cocktails and conversation, seduction and heartbreak, birthdays, weddings and funerals.

Not one of which was work.

from *Made Flesh*

Tune into this
        a line of thread
    sounding its way along   a labyrinth
        to lead you deep   deeper in
to a play of circumstance   a history
    that short-circuits in ecstasy
        a cast uncharactered

Drawn into its winding   you will spin
   a kind of spell   for flesh made word

The landscape of its happening
   is April   and a passage on a train
A flame of leaf-opening
   and a slow cadence of wire outside the window
A tongue bowing a note across a broken
   corner of tooth   and as you move
the track's percussion catches up to the beat of a
song
   that's looped in your memory all morning long
Even the beads of water weaving
   over the glass
        drop into its groove

* * *

The rain lets its fingers lift
   from the keys of concrete and new leaves
The oilspots and the gum bullets
   ground into the platform   pause
The pianist turns a page and sips his drink

And Love leaps on the train   confection-pink
   in a poof of sweater   scattering pearls
     out of her hair and clothing   cue applause

She pitches herself into a seat
   and can't seem to settle
Her foot kicking a backbeat
   to the castanet of her heart-locket
   a couple snapped into a kiss
She's a drum solo of impatience
   until her Barbie cellphone starts to plink
   Beethoven's Ninth in notes of beaten metal

"Chloe   okay okay okay   Get this
      I just had lunch with Hades   No my brother
         Half-brother really   WHAT a loser geek
We're eating right and so he says last week
      his girlfriend dumped him   left a letter
Says she's going back to her mother
      and maybe she'll see him in the fall
Then you know we do the little dance
      Oh-I'm-so-sorry   Really-no-it's-fine
and then he's getting all high-maintenance
      God I hate it when they whine

"So here I am letting him bawl
      ALL over my hot pink mohair sweater
         The one we found half-price at Cyprus mall
      What do you mean slutty   It's inviting

"But finally when he pulls himself together
      he lets on like this happens every spring
for centuries   it's some sick
      little game that they play   How rude
         is that   and now I'm not so sympathetic

"So HE starts dishing out this attitude
      I guess you're right it's just a falling-out
A falling-out I say   Whatever
      How can you have a falling out
         if you've never fallen IN   I mean
         REALLY   He's such a drama queen"

* * *

"All I wanted were the flowers
      yellow and white and wet with dew"

It was the squeak of your fingertip

slipping between the waxed petals
    that brought me swimming up to you

"They were a field of possibilities
    not open yet   I need them back
I wait by the paisley-frosted window
    holding my breath   so not to see its mist"

Each day you draw yourself closer
    as if to make your body occupy
      the least space and whatever help
    I have to offer   you resist

"When the dirt pulled like a blanket over me
    as dark as being in the blood
      I was afraid and how I clung
And the ruby-colored seeds you counted
    into my palm   at first were sweet
      until I bit them   bitter on my tongue"

Now I would take back the bait

"Now I would spit them out and never swallow"

When I offered you my arm   so smoothly
    I never thought that you would follow
spilling the flowers carelessly
    out of your lap   How could I own
      the weight of such responsibility

"Now I have outgrown the pot
    I am rootbound and desperate
      to shed my load of pollen   to explode
    in red and suicidal bud"

My heart has clotted to a chunk
    of volcanic glass   the color of a bruise
      My hands are afraid of being fists

I fret myself to arrowheads
   to flick at random into the nearest flesh
     which   when my aim holds   is yours

"The one you can't bear to keep or lose

Splinter a bone and it will mend
   stronger than ever   Scrape your skin
    and it will scar   Even the brain
   unraveling may be knit back again
But the heart   the heart is so tough
   it loves the sound of its own breaking
     It circles itself in an ever-closer
   knot of ice and glass and steel"

A kaleidoscope I never tire
   of turning over   what can hurt me
    out of reflection   what can cut me
   deep   deeply enough to heal

* * *

We are so practiced in the art
   of talking   a craft as exact and neat
as a glassblower's
          I bend to the furnace
   turn my face to the blast of heat
and dip the tip of a steel pipe
   in a bulb of soul-soft glass   I spin you
deftly   prompt you into the shape
   I want you   always at arm's length
    in a glove of woven stone   I lift you
up to my lips   empty my cheeks
   blow you like a trumpet   turning
    my own emptiness into yours
   A bubble of soap   your hope ballooning frail

Bottle of all my faults I make you
   Globe in whose reflection I
am shown swollen   the gross and callous
   ogre of a fairytale
So impatient to admire his labor
   he takes it up too soon   before
     the crystal cools   the glow still on it
   a red star whose fire's about to fail
His fingerprints are burned bald
   and still he can't keep from popping the blister
Can't help it   can't resist
   ruining everything with the slightest
    tap of a finger   only to see himself
   struck out of the cracked mirror

This isn't supposed to happen   glass
   glass is a liquid   given time
     even a window flows   like water
out of its frame   a teardrop
   taking a century to shed
What windows it claps open
   onto beauty   the sea-green tiles
    at Trinity   the bomb's white blossom
   forcing matter a moment out of its mold

Can't conversation be so clear and cold
   So spun of energy   so supple and open-
    ended   a single molecule
   stitched into itself   and always able
to start over   the injury
   defended   the slight returned in fury
Why the surrender   why do you cave in
   so quickly   collapsing like the petals
    that fold out of a blown bud
Nothing is broken   can't you see
   Nothing can ever break   our lives
    are entwined as an ivy-heavy tree
   with a galaxy put forth in every leaf

You stare at me as up the deep
   black shaft of a burrow   where
     once having hunted you   I cannot talk you
   out of   and so we come to grief

* * *

Another April   flush with spring
   we sprawl cross-legged on the lawn
     under the sycamores   we smoke
and flick the ashes   we try to talk ourselves
   out of our cigarettes   we try
to talk ourselves out of our lovers
   out of our own heads   in hope the heat
of so much conversation might
   render the matter   as fat from meat

There is a dead bird in my ear
   There is a silence and the air
     is wrapped around my temples tight
So many manners we have tried
   without a map to put ourselves aside
You solid and I solid
   striking each other   to secure
ourselves a substance   a matter more
   in clashing   than the casual clouds
     or the loose associations of the shore

How would we like a love that is not friction
   How would we like to be no more
each other's rock   or Sisyphus
   taking turns to push each other
     patiently up the slope   only to slip
and bound forever back again
   rebellious with weight and obstinate
obsidian   our knives flaked
   out of its black glass   to hack

the heart out of each other's chest
   and offer it bleeding to the sun
Who is this god we pray to   what
   Left-Handed Hummingbird do we pretend
      to priest   What floodgate of the bloodstream
   heaves open
        And stop it now   and stop

See how the pavement scintillates with ants
   carrying crumbs of dirt   and our eyes
      are fat with not weeping   the milkweed
makes froth of the grass   and we
   are firm   the effort of not yielding
      become our custom   comfort even

Oh I am sick with such heroic pity
   Oh I am tired   I would slack
Oh let my limbs transform to tree
   pounding with sap   oh let the aching
points of buds prick through my skin
   pierced inwardly   oh let me be
      a green twig   twisted and not breaking

Chris Baker (1969)

The Way's the Same

"When you have to shoot, shoot. Don't talk."
                    —*The Good, the Bad and the Ugly*

And just like Ugly Tuco says,
The way's the same in verse—
The more you talk about a thing,
The worse.

This Week in Verse

On Monday, I couldn't find a rhyme;
On Tuesday, I couldn't find the time;
On Wednesday, my printer had no ink;
On Thursday, I visited my shrink;
On Friday, I had a dinner date;
On Saturday, I slept in too late;
On Sunday, I watched my favorite shows;
Come Monday, I think I'll switch to prose.

One Last Request

When I was a young man, hard headed and full of pride,
I got a pretty girl pregnant and asked her to be my bride.
Then I went to my best friend to see if he'd be my best man.
I never thought I'd see them holding each other's hands.

I said, "Hey there, friend—she's to be my wife.
And those lipstick stains are going to cost someone their life."
Tequila and jealousy, mixed in with a gun
Changed all of our lives while killing one.

My son, you're twenty-one, and it's time for you to know
The true story of what happened twenty years ago.
This man's not your uncle, in fact, he's my best friend.
But he's been like a brother with this secret since way back when.

Now son, your mother, she was a good woman.
But we never married and I ain't proud of what I've done.
When I was a young man, I made my place in Hell.
I shot your mother and buried her in the corn where she fell.

So, one last request before I go, look in my eyes—they're sober and sane.
I've done my best but I still have regrets; I've lost more than I've gained.
So, please spread my ashes over the corn in an endless green Iowa field.
And if I was a good man, we'll see it in what the harvest yields.

Jeremy Jerrell

It was just an old guitar
And even older songs
That Jeremy Jerrell played those nights
While we all sang along.

Some had a glass of beer,
Some had a bit of weed,
And Jeremy drank and smoked them all,
He lived the partyer's creed.

He knew how to pick those strings,
He knew how to sing those songs,
He never stopped drinking and smoking while playing
And we all sang along.

Some of his songs kicked ass,
And some of them were sad,
But all his songs were from deep inside
And he sang them with all he had.

We wondered how he lived
By playing and singing songs.
But once he tuned his cheap guitar,
We had to sing along.

We loved the way he looked,
All alone with his guitar.
Any of us would've traded an arm
To be the star of the bar.

The men played air guitar,
The women moved their hips.
(And more than a few had loved Jeremy
With much more than their lips.)

And strangers bought him drinks,
And musicians were amazed,
And everyone loved Jeremy Jerrell,
But those were simpler days.

And then we all got older,
And couldn't frequent that bar,
And we stopped hearing our favorite songs
He played on his guitar.

We never really knew him.
Did we look him in the eye?
We never sat and talked with him.
Did we even say goodbye?

It was just an old guitar
And even older songs
That Jeremy Jerrell played those nights
As we all sang along.

A Prostitute's Reply to a Pimp

"Come live with me and be my love"

When opportunity has knocked,
The door is opened or kept locked.
I've got to think your offer through
Before I go to work for you.

Time strips the youth from one who tries
To make a buck unzipping flies.
The johns pay best when you are young
And had no manhood on your tongue

When you're eighteen, your knees are sturdy;
By twenty-one, they're scarred and dirty.
And as you age, you'll get less dates
And end up lowering your rates.

What happens when you're thirty-one?
The pimps will tell you, it's been fun.
They'll take you off their favorite street,
And then go find another treat.

Now that I've thought your offer through,
I think that I should answer you.
Though opportunity has knocked,
I think I'll keep my deadbolt locked.

Since half the world is filled with pricks,
I'll turn a profit turning tricks.
May all your family jewels turn blue
Before I go to work for you.

Anniversary

"The grave's a fine and private place,
But none, I think, do there embrace."
–Andrew Marvell, "To His Coy Mistress"

Great Time, some say, always devours
The smallest ants and superpowers.
Some say they need to seize the day
Before their crimson lust turns gray.
Some search the street, some search the net
For Mister Stud or Miz Coquette.
Who dares to look for Mr. Right
In bars or discos late at night?
With flashing eyes, he'll turn you on;
But, by tomorrow, he'll be gone.
He'll never write, he'll never call—
Last night was just another ball.
Young surfers surf in cyberspace
Searching for lovers who'll replace
Those frozen nymphs with teasing eyes
Who flash the world with open thighs.
And chatrooms post erotic themes
That show her fonts, but not her dreams.
Dear Mr. Wrong and Ms. Right-Now,
Your milk is sour, why buy your cow?
If you go out and do above
You'll cheat yourself with shallow love.
You'll live as if you're in high school
When carpe diem was way cool.
Yet it's naive for one to think
Life holds a glass without a drink;
And know that it's the tallest tale
For one to smoke and not inhale.
Forget a love that's sweet and pure,
You'll need a love that can endure
An age or two or maybe more—
Eternity's a fractal shore.

The grasses grow, its roots wrap round
Our huddled coffins underground.
In thirty thousand years, they'll rot
And let the earth reclaim this spot.
And when that happens, we may trust
Those worms to move our mortal dust.
Our souls will rest till time allows
Our bodies to renew their vows.
All flesh and bone await rebirth;
All flesh and bone become new earth.
For love outlasts time's endless coil,
Love lies beyond the blackest soil.
When science binds our telomeres,
We'll live for several hundred years.
And if we've found a single heart,
Six hundred years won't make us part.
But we may want our final rites
To stop the trade of days and nights.
And if we do, we'll find a day
And time that we will pass away.
The grave's a sure and final place,
Where two, I know, will there embrace.

Bill Coyle (1968)

Like many of my contemporaries, I began writing in free verse. Even then, however, I was obsessed with questions of form—where to break the line, how many lines to have in a given strophe, and so on. My discovery of Auden was the road-to–Damascus-experience that ended my free-verse period. I read his Selected Poems more times than I can count, and when the cover fell off, I framed it and hung it over my desk. Other influences followed, chief among them Louis MacNeice, James Merrill, Anthony Hecht, Richard Wilbur, Philip Larkin, C. H. Sisson, Derek Walcott, A. D. Hope, Geoffrey Hill and Derek Mahon.

Why does form appeal to me? First, I love the music it makes. I'm a frustrated musician, and meter and rhyme allow me to bring rhythm, melody and harmony into my writing. Second, I like the fact that others, non-poets included, hear and appreciate this music. Third, form is an addictive pleasure—a technical challenge that is at the same time thrilling and meditative. Fourth and finally (and I hope not too pretentiously) writing in meter is, for me, a statement of faith, an assertion that there is an ordering principle beneath the surface of things, and that it wants us to be happy.

Though I loosen things up every now and again, my use of form is relatively traditional and my syllable count fairly strict. I do, however, see each new poem as a formal experiment, an opportunity to use meters or rhyme schemes I haven't tried before, or to express something new in a familiar form.

The Magic Circle

1.   Autumn

Early this morning I glanced out the window
and saw her underneath the maple tree.
She was as pale as that white gown of hers.
Hard to believe it's been a year already.
I waved. She turned away, paused for a moment,

then walked into the mist that marked the border
between my backyard and what lay beyond.
Proserpine, I called, but she was gone.
I am convinced that this was Proserpine
and not, as Mrs. Grandison maintains,
some nut escaped from the state hospital.
All Hallow E'en approaches. Skeletons
hang from the trees along my street and ghosts,
emboldened, haunt the front yards in broad daylight.

2.   Winter

The swallows sleep beneath the river ice.
The salamanders whisper in the fire.
Hermes Trismestigus' new work is open
at one of its obscurer passages,
of which there are intolerably many.
I take a break to watch the local news.
Toward midnight, I collect my charts and go
to make my nightly survey of the heavens.
Mercifully they're still there. One of the saddest
developments I've witnessed in my time
has been astrology's decline from science
to fortune telling of the basest sort,
its long eclipse by disciplines that measure
not meaning, now, but distance, size and mass...
As if mere matter mattered in itself.

3.   Spring

Bears wake from their long hibernation, now,
hirsute initiates with tales to tell
to those with ears to listen. Proserpine
returns as well, and Christ. And may not I?
The budding trees and the returning birds
figure the transmigration of the soul
so beautifully I wish that I could die
and see the world again through infant eyes.

I intimate these things to Ed, my mailman,
who nods politely. Ed is not about
to jeopardize his Christmas tip (last year
an old tin can transmuted into gold)
regardless how much of a character
he and the other villagers may think me.

4.   Summer

Little did I know when I concocted
my potion that, although one may stop time,
it is impossible to turn it back.
Youth, they say, is wasted on the young.
Perhaps I'll have a tee-shirt made that reads,
Eternal life is wasted on the old.
And yet the world is no less beautiful.
Toward evening dew collects upon the lawn,
rising again as fireflies. Above
the white New England church a flock of swallows
copies a Greek text out in Arabic,
and in the maple trees a light breeze stirs,
sounding for all the world like water falling
distantly off the edges of the world.

Leave Taking
i.m. Sten Söderström

The dead, we say, are the departed. They
pass on, they pass away, they leave behind
family, friends, the whole of humankind—
They have gone on before. Or so we say.

But could it be the opposite is true?
Now, as I stand here in the graveled drive
at moonrise, unaccountably alive,
I have the sense that it is we, not you,

who are departing, spun at breakneck speed
through space and time, while you stay where you are—
intimate of dark matter and bright star—
and watch the brilliant, faithless world recede.

Perspectives

i.

Hardy, in his great poem "Hap," maintains
he would be comforted to find his pains

were not what they in fact appear to be—
expected outcomes of "Crass Casualty"—

but the fulfillment of some higher will
intent on doing Thomas Hardy ill.

ii.

Aneas, faced with overwhelming odds,
saw in a vision how the very gods

whom he had servèd now helped his foes destroy
the walls and towers and palaces of Troy.

There is in Vergil, though, no evidence
this vision comforted the Trojan prince.

The Flautist of North Station

The flautist of North Station,
playing Amazing Grace,
will get, for compensation,
some quarters in a case

on which, for sympathy,
he's taped a picture of

his daughters, so that we
may see he plays for love;

may see he plays for free,
while someone in a suit
takes up the melody
our man plays on the flute

and starts to whistle it
as he departs the station,
bound for a world unfit
for any such salvation.

Jill Alexander Essbaum (1971)

Rarely do I begin writing in form. The first drafts spill out straight from the mouth of the muse—if I dare admit such a thing happens. But that's just step one. Most of the real writing is done in the rewriting (steps two through forty-eight, if I'm lucky). When a poem isn't working, my instinct is always to put it into a form, any form. To change the shape of it so that the mysteries within can find their way out. I'm completely hypnotized by rhyme. Rhyme is easy on the ears and I'm drawn to the cadence of words. A simple rhyme beats a forced rhyme any day, though I am guilty of both. Poems at their cores are songs, so whether formally metered or not, there's got to be some musicality to them, some kind of tempo.

Writers who don't toy around with sound and meter and shape and syllable and line, miss out on what secrets the poem may be withholding. If you listen, the poem itself will (often) tell you what it wants to look like, how it wants to be written. My job as the person whose name appears underneath the last stanza is to do what I can to allow that to happen. And ultimately, when I don't let the poem room to be and to breathe, when I find myself desperately wrenching Meaning (capital M) out of it, I'm dooming it to failure, to an early and painful death. But form keeps me honest. It's far clearer to me when I'm too much in the way of the words when they are bound to a certain architecture.

Wednesday, Ash

Nothing of me will survive.
This body that I wear will die
and my mouth—nevermind its loveliness—
is set to shut itself into a sorrow the size

of restlessness and lack.
The lips go too. They slack
at the corners crying *no, no*
but still they go. They do not talk back.

And then for every finger I have counted on—

so many times—there is a going, and a gone.
They leave to rest in pieces with once sad and pretty
    hands of grief
waiting for an Easter dawn

(which no one hears approaching when they're buried
    underneath the ground).
And my feet cannot quit thinking quickstep, swing, the sound
of toe taps or a waltz. *Hush.* No dancing for the dead.
The ball is done. The slipper? *Nowhere to be found.*

And my belly, full or no is quiet.
Then it will feast as a ghost feasts—on nothing, a diet
of sediment, sleep, a lily or two.
I shall not fuss, I shall not make riot

or rivalry any, *any* more. The eyes are vacant, tenantless,
for they have been plucked out. Relentless
death, you have withered shut my heart
like an old rose closing, pungent and motionless

in the closet of the rats and of the bones. Everything I am is dust,
or shadows of it, clay unkissed.
Having died in the desert, I do not come back.
Having died in the desert, it is the drought I miss.

How can that *be*? Nothing, nothing of us survives.
Every inch of us will die,
and not a thing that God can do will stop it.
Even Christ, the very self of God was crucified

and dead three days, entombed.
Angels wept as little children, women loomed
about His bloody, broken body swaddled in a shroud.
And then—He rose. Like Lazarus or bread, or any bright moon

which lifts as thunder over mountaintops and homes.
Like that, my God—save me, save me from the groan

and creak of a coffin's rusty hinge
and resurrect us all, one by one—

all the bodies that no longer breathe or move,
and every soul that reaches but cannot grasp the thing it loves.
Save us to a grace we cannot ever hope to understand,
such that in our dyings—behold—*somehow?*—we live.

Concerning the Ends of Us

After Jonathan Edwards

It's the devil in me I suppose,
or the damsel slope of my aristocratic nose
or the earthquakes coming of my every prayer
to rumble and throb at the epicenter of all doubt, but year

after year I make these promises:
I will be a Good Enough, says
me, I will be kind to children,
and slack off the booze and act with Christian

fortitude all times, all ways. Damn if I don't go curly trying.
Attempts aside, forget it. I'm dying
of a malady named *egocitosis*,
and you are too—the self shifts

shimmy like a snake into the corners
sanctified as *soul*. And it lingers
there, and multiplies like cancer or a hutch
of Easter rabbits. The heart, which

isn't immune to anything, turns numb to all
others, dumb as the muscle that it is, and Hell
is where the sickest of us go to colonize
as lepers far away from Heaven's well. If I

know this, it's because I've seen it in a dream.
God, who from the earth seems
so regal to us, austere
as Solomon, doesn't care

where we wind up in the end.
It's not that He's no good. Rather, God depends
on nothing save but God. And we are zero added
but the glory of God's own bad-

assed idea to call us made. Still, we barter with the Him
each day, begging *Sir, the hem
of your garment and I will be fit
to be whole, or close to it*

at least—as if by this God's joy is secure.
Not that there isn't hope of course. The sure
way to paradise is turn right at the tree
and keep your eyes shut up like the knees

of a virgin lest the luscious fruit be tempting.
Then, it's not called sinning,
it's called getting by. And if we do it just so,
when we die our maker calls us to the throne

and we shall sit there eternities long
as jesters in the courts of a king
who is far independent of us. And the soul
we keep pristine as sculptor's ice is well,

and our spirits ever in the eyesights of the Father,
whose cataract gaze is like bruises left by water.

Death Song

The darkness mumbled *earthquake*
and I could not help but go.
under that black weakness,
I couch against my soul

(or what is left of it
beneath the rubble and the moan).
Grief remits to eulogize
the whimper in my bones

and I am painful as
the ache of open wounds
and their disease.
Dying comes more soon

than I can beg it not
to venture. It is not good,
this scheming anguish,
is unknown even to God,

or so it seems. Some nights
I think I see it in the fret
of my own eyes singed
with sad fire, a last regret

still regretting herself.
If I could be certain the prize
of death is paradise
I might organize

some belief to ease me
through *these hours*, extending
so vastly that infinite threads
could be woven of their rending.

Hotel Infinity

In my Father's house there are many mansions.

Shall I procure a room for us, or me alone?
Who knows who I'll be doing when the trumpet blows

and the grand last call is shouted from wherever Heaven
deems to be, and every good spirit shouts *Land of Canaan*

Here I Come! Do I need to make a reservation?
Could be quite the scandal, *hmm*? Who shall be forsaken

and who shall be redeemed? Not a saint will know
until the time to die arrives and *off we go*

to a far and unseen planet where all rooms face east.
That, so when we wake to death we are, at the very least,

fortified, eager to rise, rise with the sun and every angel
blinking lively eyes and all wings against the light's auspicious swell,

oh conundrum city. What if I can't manage underneath the feathers?
Worse, what if I'm unwelcome there, like hurricane weather

beating on the sheen, glass sands of Paradise's beach? *I cannot worry details
just this now.* I've luggage to pack, have the mail

put on hold and then to lay up treasure starting at this moment.
With any luck, the new wine pressed *vintage me* will take to ferment

into something good and grain.
It is the tale of the chaff and the wheat again,

some to keep, and some to throw off to the birds, away.
Until, I wait ready as virgins are for the day

when Jesus' very brawny arms will hold us.
If it were not so—*wouldn't he have told us?*

Cemetery Road

I walk through the city as if in my sleep
but the road sobers me. On the left,
an unlocked gate and graves in disrepair.
I hear the shambling away of sinister footfalls.
I smell the char of an untended fire.
Behind the very last of many broken headstones,
a fig tree. Wooden. Bare.

The soil is like glass when I touch it. A sun
is wasted in the sky. From this tree, learn its lesson:
for fruit that feeds and grows full in imminent
sunlight, there are other harvests germinating
in darkness, equally impending. Out from the earth
comes good things to eat. Wise in the ground,
good things are eaten away.

Into hands unknown, my spirit is condemned.
I will grow into a black pear, globular
and entwined by long tendrils and a cardioclast sorrow.
A vinedresser will cut away what might have been
my bounty. He will feed me to his animals.
Wild wheat and christ-thorn will spring up
from my burned and bitter seeds.

Despair

I become despair
in remembrance
of your hair—

the black feel of it
against my inner thigh,
skimming my clit

(*oh*) as you brushed past
on your pilgrimage
to my breast—

now tell—*which did you love best?*

Fissure

If skeleton is something more,
it is the architecture of bone—
a marvel fabricating mischief,
grunting come and groaning go.
Ossify this, old patriarch.
I wave mostly with my toes.

Metatarsically designed
like the butterfly's proboscis,
they are coiled when in disuse.
Funny God, someday you'll miss us—
mandible, tibia, cranium, me—
the joke is in the humerus,

but won't you laugh the day I die?
The marrow and the clavicle
will deprecate, and worms to feast.
Then I'll sing you in the temple
of my carcass, critically.
Corpus criminy: spectacle.

Ply your physio-origami,
fold me up in awkward fashions.
Promise me a rainbow only
when the weather turns commotion.
Forge a rib or sternum from
this disbeliever's apprehension,

and the doubt lodged in my skull.
Anatomically yours, signed Jill.

Jenny Factor (1969)

I came by verse form the old fashioned way—in a childhood that was apprenticed figuratively to poetry and literally to a great teacher, Myra Cohn Livingston. As poet-in-my-school, Myra took us through iambs and dactyls, quatrains and tetrameters, the use of the refrain, but above all how to see the world through the special glass of simile and metaphor. The arts were in the schools back then. I worked hard at sharpening and studying the poet's toolkit.

When I was seven years old, with an inflated sense of my own importance, I explained to my parents that I was put on the earth to unlock the poems in everything. I still remember the sensation. I felt poems moving under objects, swimming in a space underneath the time-space of the concrete world. I'd walk, dragging my finger along the edge of a chain link fence, feeling the rhythm in my body, looking around, trying to unwind the poems in the things I was looking at. Already, those poems had forms I could almost imagine.

I'm describing here a poem's *shape*. What I don't mean is its *verse form*. If poems, especially unwritten poems, have a shape for me, it's simply because they do (and because they don't, like prose, wander along discovering endlessly, without outer edges like a galaxy). I generally write in my head, trying different tools, until I can chisel the poem out.

Unraveling at the Name, my first book, tells something of a story about a dis-assembling life. In *Unraveling*, verse form acts as the guardrail on the staircase down, the crumbs on the trip into the forest. Luckily, I'd picked up and practiced those parts of my toolkit, or I couldn't have shaped the story as it wanted to be told.

I care about shapes. I like shapely poems. But I don't care about labels like new formalism. I feel blessed that contemporary poetry has and will continue to have a plurality of styles. In my experience as a person and poet, the life stuff often starts precisely where the labels leave off.

Summer Journal, Israel (Age 19)

After work, we'll hit the kibbutz beach.
The whole group tans together, half-undressed.
I write it all in letters home to Lise:
My bunkmate, Val, might be a lesbian.
My keenest crush is Sean, an older man,
bandanna'd, dimpled chin, and cute, but married.

So horny-crazed, I bet I'll never marry;
that day we drink warm beers out on the beach—
Sean and I. A skinny Kenyan man
offers me ten dollars to undress
for him. Sure I could be a lesbian
but only if I were trying it with Lise.

I save each letter I get back from Lise.
One week, her roommate sophomore year gets married.
The next, she drives her aunt, a lesbian,
to the family cottage by the beach.
And do I have her new address?
And please do tell about those men!

And so I write her how a young French man—
brilliant, fine-boned, with an aunt named Lise—
and I went swimming naked. We undressed
under stars, butt-drunk and making merry,
among the jellyfish and wave-washed beach,
till Val came out and watched (that lesbian!).

Lise knows for certain she's no lesbian,
although she's never liked it with a man,
I tell Val as we walk out to the beach.
I'm sure Val must be gay, I write to Lise,
because she says she never wants to marry
and doesn't shave (I see when she's undressed).

The night Sean kissed me in my Spanish dress,

he said he used to date a lesbian
some years before he and his wife got married,
and once he'd even made love to a man!
We drank some Scotch. I showed him Lise's
picture. Our footprints watermarked the paper beach,

and then I wondered if I'd marry, beach,
reach shore? *Am I lesbian? A man?*
Wind blew my dress. I stood. I thought of Lise.

Extramarital…

Scotch and Soda

The front door slipped from its latch and he
came in—the man you're married to and love.
He knows about this "us," this you-and-me,
and it is for his sake that words like "love"
and "tomorrow" don't flow between us easily;
when Ella slips into the groove on the CD
player, your shirt lifts above your head
(my ice settling in my glass, I feel sour beads
of sweat from the summer heat rising
on my skin). Here the truth is surprising
even to me: I don't mind what we *don't*
say, what you *can't* feel. "I love you" is scary.
I mean something lighter. What I want:
Lay with me, wide-eyed, wary.

Rubyfruit

You kissed my mouth as if it were my sex
before you kissed me everywhere, before
that night in Rubyfruit's, my glasses off,
the room elided, darkness stretched, a blur
zip-studded by red pinlights, hemmed and held

a cloth we had no future written on.
Around us, well-dressed women stirred the darkness
as they walked. The bar's cold black streak streamed
past willows, necks swayed in to sup and speak.
I learned the map of textures on your cheek.
Benched near the place where others knit limbs, lives,
my body's affirmation—a surprise—
to our established friendship. You confessed—
amazing humming of my flesh's yes.

Playing Doctor

Yes, my love, I'm yours. I'll give myself
over to your teasing, tender care
to let you open me, deliberate,
your hand, a scientist, whose probing dares
to peel the blossom budded thirty years
in silence. I wake like a newborn, tears
of trust and outrage, wet and cold and bared.
What will be born of us when you have dared
to lift my fetal, embryonic heat
toward your nipples on my floral sheets?
What climax will our drumming raise us toward?
When we make love, new love, what will be made?
In that place, exposed, exhausted, laid,
if I'm with you, I will not feel afraid.

"Now What Can We Do for My Pretty?" You Ask....

Sometimes I touch my breasts and think of you.
Sometimes, as if my body were your own
private kingdom, I don't want my own
hands to touch myself after you
leave the room. It's like you lock me from myself
by going away. Inside my insides,
I am half-awake, half-opened. From your side

of New York, the Great Woods, you check your shelf
for potions, ivories, hairpieces, sleek combs
to knit my hair around when you return.
Oh mistress, busy worldly woman, turn
the bolt; return to me; set your combed
nape in my lap. Kiss me till the fine
evening turns a deep flush, like your skin, mine.

Misapprehension

I don't want you always to act your age:
Fall apart a little for me please,
so when I kiss your mouth, your brow, your creamy
arms, your downy neck, eyelids, your strange
intense dark copper-lidded eyes that close
against me, when I hold you till your whole
strut-length of spine releases to my holding,
when I lay you, stroke your guiltless rose
open toward me, ages overturned...
I don't want you to act your age, just yearn
toward what I offer; soften to my touch,
let me reach the place where you give milk,
suck and tongue you till my touch is much,
much more than youth or age or silk on silk.

Adrift

Curled up in my arms like a small boy,
you took my breast into your hungry lips
and met my eye and smiled, nursing child,
and cried into my lap when you had come
too many times for your skin to endure
more touch, and cried and cried till you were done
while I said, *Si si si*, as to my son's
despondent nighttime-waking. Dream-wracked, dear,
your rosy body swam through sweetness, tears

on the black sheets of your bed in the ambient light
of two candles. Like a ship sailing to a shore
we've never reached before, we sailed each other
leg over leg, your back washed up against my breasts
till your son's door opened and we dressed.

Safer Sex?

So no more nipples? (Post-lactation leak.)
And winter comes like sandpaper to lips
which now keep their chaste distance from my lips.
Of course my palm may stroke your nether cheek
as long as I wear gloves for full descent
into the place you want my dig and thrust.
Sex, you call this. I say, lack of trust.
You say I'm inching toward an argument.
I call your latex, Safe Sex for the Heart.
I want to find your mouth on me, the taste
of you, familiar, moving with my tongue.
You've come. Neglected, handled, and unstrung,
I stay in bed and watch you dress in haste.
I've lost more than one sense without your taste.

Confidential P. S.

So now when we make love, what have we made?
Not "life," although our blossoming belies
a simple definition of mere breath
and heartbeat. Surely something is implied
we do not make: not home, not spouse, not child
(though sometimes I am yours or you are mine
in ways that seem to posit us *en womb*).
When others speak of loving to create
a life, we know we'll never share a room
for more than hours running. Yes. I mind
this making time by time and lay by lay

a stay against the current of our days.
Real work that moves no rivers. Mother, wife,
we live out elsewhere. Love knitting no life.

Happenstance

My neighbor's garden's shaped by oddball love:
spare tires planted with hibiscus blooms,
a fairy circle sprouting up in bulbs,
the grass a mass of weeded happenstance.

Spare tires—planted with hibiscus—bloom
like perfect testaments to making-use,
while grass, a weeded mass, by happenstance
pops up white and purple pixie heads.

Like perfect testaments to making-use,
nests fill night lanterns, nesting boxes, trees.
Newborn sparrows lift their pixie heads.
A little boy runs through a square of reeds.

Nests fill night lanterns, nesting boxes, trees.
Fecundity is everywhere I look.
A little boy runs through a square of reeds
as if he's acting out a children's book.

Fecundity is everywhere I look.
Good use is made of every accident
in family-planted gardens. Children's books
are seldom whimsy-riddled as these nooks.

Good use. How can they make of accident
a happy beauty? I am so confused.
Whimsy poses riddles in these nooks.
Life's not about what's given, but what's used.

Such happy beauty leaves me here, confused
inside a fairy circle made of bulbs:
my life—much given, sometimes little used,
set in this garden, shaped by oddball love.

Song Beside a Sippy Cup

In the never truly ever
truly dark dark night, ever
blinds-zipped, slat-cut,
dark-parked light,
you (late) touch my toes
with your broad flat own
horny-nailed cold toes.
Clock-tock, wake-shock.

In the ever truly never
truly long long night, our
little snoring-snarling
wild-child mild-child
starling-darling wakes every
two, three (you-sleep) hours,
in the never truly ever
truly lawn brawn fawn dawn.

Réunion À Deux

If anybody errs, it will be you.
Don't tell me stories that later you'll deny,
or brag of your affairs now that we're through.
I only told you what you asked me to.
Would you prefer that I recant or lie
when everything you heard is true?
If anybody errs, it will be you.
What crime could I be charged with in reply?
I told you just what you asked me to.

If anybody errs, it will be you.
Not I. Not I. Not I. Not I. Not I.

While Undressing…

Boys are all right. I have a thing for *girls*
Their dresses are a festive celebration.

Silk or flannel, girls are what I *like*
My vice acts out in any situation.

One glance at women's hands is liable *to*
tumble me toward vain infatuation.

A girl's jeans zipper beckons me to *pull*
and coax the tongue to fabric separation.

I'm partial to girls' napes of necks and *their*
haircuts, long or short. Each alteration

causes fresh astonishment. Short *skirts*—
their skittish hemlines dance a demarcation

summoning my eyes to follow *down*
the length of leg, imagine exploration

with tongue and lips and hands. I would far *rather*
soft upper arms, light licks, the levitation

of thin hairs in a breeze on calves and nipples *than*
waste my tongue in witty conversation.

So Woman let your blue eyes throw me *over*
leonine and slow. This titillation

must lead to yes and yes and there and *their*
to skin on skin with no more hesitation

as hot tongues tease two shy and slippery *heads!*
to healthy heat. Sing praise! Sing exultation!

Riqueza

> *Tengo la dicha fiel/y la dicha perdida:*
> *la una coma rosa,/la otra coma espina...*
> Gabriela Mistral

Although the Eaton Wash was pink with ghost
and dust, I took the horsy path again
down to where the water and the rain
meet. My toes are happiest when placed
where specks of guppies cluster light and tumble
water on my skin up to my ankles.
Moss in brackish eddy rides the ripples.
Sparrows dart away from me like troubles.
Sagey, dusty, doggy smell of trail
drags my body back to what is real:
I have a faithful joy and a joy that is lost.

The night you flew twenty hours home from Oman, got
Sam to sleep, we sat on the kitchen floor,
blasted with a clear domestic light,
and I told you I couldn't stay married anymore.
We took our regal bands from our ring fingers
but your wouldn't budge—knuckles outsized joints.
Was the Divine Jester making points?
Perhaps. We ended at the sink—in blood, cold water,
I holding your whole body from behind.
Although it didn't imply change, it implied,
I have been faithful, Joy. I have been lost.

Mommy, can't we have "old family" back?
I want you and my dad to live together.

Is Grandpa Andy really Daddy's father?
Are *hot* and *cold* or *east* and *beast* a match?
Why can't I make the video in my head
play only good dreams? Mommy, don't help.
Mom, you're the best mom in the whole world!
Look, I poured the milk out by myself.
Do you miss me when I'm at my dad's?
How come you have my helmet but not my knee pads?
I have a faithful joy and a joy that is lost.

Eaton Wash. I walked there with my love.
Eaton Wash. I dreamed there of another.
One who'd gnaw my insides like a bone.
One who'd tease my tears out like a mother.
One I wanted till my nipples milked.
Dusk spinning with life inside her room,
cranky, cunning, keen insightful talk
in that garden overrun with bloom.
Moments would expand there like a lung.
Raw, uncertain, realizing, unstrung,
I am unfaithful, Joy, but far from lost.

Echo the perfect conquest of the sea
over every groomed, tamed, patient shore.
Stitch a salvaged piece of what I've torn
into the quilt my son keeps on his knee.
Rich with purple martins, rich with sparrow,
live oak, flat bush, goldfinch, tufted brown
stream birds that dart off from me close to ground.
I am as rich with purple as with sorrow.
Thirty-one, an acorn, dropped, reborn,
resting on the dust (or stone) exhaust.
Oh how loved is the rose, how loving the thorn!
I have a faithful joy and a joy that is lost.

Ted Genoways (1972)

The poets I most admired in my early reading—and still return to—were mostly the poets who broke from the formalism of the 1950s. I read James Wright, William Stafford, Robert Bly, Philip Levine, and many of their free verse heirs. Over time, however, I noticed that each of these poets began with first books of strict iambic pentameter and often what I responded to most in their poems was what Annie Finch has dubbed "the ghost of meter." About the same time I came to this realization, I began discovering English-language poets from other countries, especially Seamus Heaney, Derek Walcott, and Tony Harrison. Their poems excited me, because they still contained the natural rhythm of speech within regulated meters. More than four hundred years ago, Montaigne described this perfectly: "Just as sound, when pent up in the narrow channel of a trumpet, comes out sharper and stronger, so it seems to me that a thought, when compressed into the numbered feet of poetry, spring forth much more violently and strikes me a much stiffer jolt." I like this especially because Montaigne is not advocating prettifying the language; just the opposite. I, too, find that when I force my own narrative tendencies into meter and rhyme that the language grows denser and richer, that I veer less into prosaic detail and more toward poetic compression. By the same token, I try to remember Montaigne's own counterbalance: "I am not one of those who think that a good rhythm makes a good poem.... if the inventions are pleasant, if wit and judgment have done their work well, I shall say: There is a good poet, but a bad versifier." I always prefer good free verse to bad formalism. I don't write in form for any other reason than it helps me to create poems more satisfying to my own ear.

Outside the Slaughterhouse

Some nights, following the interstate home,
I pull off at the stockyards to hear the drone
of butchering. The floodlight casts shadows
across the catwalk and the feedlot below.
Calves look up from their pens, eyes like polished
stones. In the distance, the Missouri twists
in its bed. This is where my grandfather,

sleepless nights, walked the banks; where water
turned red by sundown. Here, he scooped slit guts,
sawed bones. Here, the river's dull force still cuts.
The moon's crescent curves like a gambrel hook.
Clouds stall like freighted cattle cars. I stoop
to fill my pockets with rocks, cold and worn.
These too were mountains before I was born.

The Killing Floor

> . . .and so out of each pen there rolled a steady stream of carcasses,
> which the men on the killing-floor had to get out of the way.
> —*Upton Sinclair,* The Jungle

I. The Drover

*Theodore Thompson Genoways, Omaha Union Stockyards, after
sundown, November 11, 1932*

Snow furls through the floodlights' potassium flicker,
rides the wash of cattle cars, as they pitch and boom
past the switch to the yards. He squats in a slicker

and hip boots by a fire licking from an oil drum.
After the engineer sounds *all clear,* boys scramble
down rail ties, hooking then rolling back the side doors,

snug against their ramps, yelling and clanging handbells.
When the Burlington westbound clacks the trestleworks—
tracks buckling, rumbling timbers—the drover lowers

his head, then lifts the prod from the coals, smoke billow
trailing to where he pulls the gate open. Cow hooves, worn
smooth, slip on the chute's wet grate. They trip and roll

or slide on their fore-knees. Crowded pinbone to horn,
they shoulder through doors, sprawl like newborns in the mud.

High over the yard, sleepless in his cot, Ted starts

when his brother, the drover, shouts. Flailing, hot-prod
charring their sides, cattle kick till they jump, then trot
on hobbled legs into the maze of the feedlots.

II. Moonshining

The boardinghouse roof, past midnight, November 12, 1932

All October, Johannsen slipped cobs of white corn
in the pockets of his smock, to fill two tow sacks
stashed under his bunk. At night, fresh from the kill-floor,

he dipped his fist in troughs or picked the fodder box
of a hog pen for ears, then—while playing poker—
he cupped his mortar and pestle like a soup bowl,

grinding kernels to meal. Now he seals the cooker
and stokes the fire. No one talks, waiting till it boils.
Each dawn, Ted watches this man lift an iron maul

and shout. When the steer lurches into the chute, bowed
like a beggar, he strikes so the sledge splits the skull.
They drop and shudder. Whatever breed, bull or cow,

they buckle to their knees and groan. Their red tongues loll
and jerk like dogs in summer, neck muscles knotted
and twitching. Johannsen smiles when the cooker taps.

The copper coil—packed in a tub of snow—sputters
and drips into the pail. Johannsen dips his cup
under the nipple and takes a long, thoughtful sip.

He settles the mug into Cullen's hand. Blinded
drinking coolant strained through day-old bread, Cullen pulls
a chain all day, sending carcasses down the line

when the cutters call. They wait for his approval—
to take the first drink and grin—before filing by
filling their tins. In a few hours, these same men—tanked

on high shot—will stand side by side on the cut line,
Johannsen swinging the maul, the moon still hanging
full-white and cratered as the face of an angus.

III. The Bird-catcher

The boardinghouse, daybreak, November 12, 1932

On the docks below Ted's window, stacks of feed hay
rot, riddled with weevils. He watches a fowler,
crouched in rushes by river's edge, hug a ten-gauge,

waiting for mallards to set down. Every hour
since Wallace's boots clambered down the stairs, heavy
as hooves, he has risen again from the same dream

to find the same birder stock-still, but his bevy
grown—a row of headless ducks strung up by their feet
and bleeding out onto the snow and trampled reeds.

He draws the blind. When Wallace returns, wages blown,
drunk and still stinking of blood, Ted must yield the bunk—
its bedsprings spent and sagging with the constant stone

of sleep—to kick the streets till his shift bell is rung.
His eyes comb the yellow stains on his ceiling,
the way a practiced helmsman can sound river depths

or a heron spear a wriggling fish—by reading
ripples for snags or trout. His father always said
Cast toward the center, where bubbles broke and spread

on the dawn-reddened lake, *then watch your cork wobble.*
Wait till it jerks, wait till you see it go under.
The shotgun cracks and repeats, its echoed double

coming like a clear reflection off the water.
Ted peers through a keyhole in the curtains in time
to see: a flock of pintails flap into the air,

the fowler's dog tread against the current, the line
of dockworkers turn from burning wheat and cheer.
And his brother's boots start their slow climb up the stairs.

IV. Rendering

Outside the Swift Slaughterhouse, noon, November 12, 1932

Cutters pour from the slaughterhouse doors to the catwalk
above the lot. They lean on the handrail, chewing
crusts smeared with lard, or flop and roll their bloody smocks

into pillows and drowse in the sun. Smoke, spewing
from twin stacks, chokes the yard with the stench of burnt hooves.
Johannsen wets his lips and hands Cullen the flask.

His frosted eyes jitter from the boardinghouse roof
to the tracks below, where a low-riding stake truck
brakes by a frozen calf. Ted squints, his stare fixed

on the workman, untying the tarp of his rig.
When he peels the canvas back, Johannsen elbows
Cullen and says, *Look-it*: dead cows piled three-high, legs

grey and stiff as tipped sawhorses. When early snows
blew in, tracks drifted under dunes, cattle guards sank,
and mavericks wandered the switchyard, snow-blind and lost.

Drovers chained dead calves to the axle by their shanks—

tires chawing mud, gearshift rasping between first
and reverse—until each body would crackle and twist

like an uprooted stump. Now, through the brute silence
blanketing the yard, the workman's hacksaw sings across
the calf's hock like the bow to some grim violin.

He scoops each hoof into a sack and shrouds the carcass
with canvas, to warm in the sun. The shift bell rings
and men shamble through the doors, down the grated stairs,

to the kill-floor. Ted guides Cullen back to his chain
and pulley, watching how his eyes jump, when steers
rush the chute. Johannsen yells and swings the hammer.

V. Horn

Swift Slaughterhouse, sundown, November 12, 1932

Bone-crush and moan. Over the rattle of hoist chains
lifting gates, Johannsen yells *next!* before the dead bulls
even slump to the shackle trap, the gambrel-man

cuffing each at the hock. The bulls jerk when he pulls
the lever, heaved into the air till the roller
rests in the trolley track. They twist, strung like linen

in a spring breeze, blood and spume drizzling the kill-floor.
One night on the boardinghouse roof, the gambrel-man
whispered, *I seen it, Ted. Knocked a hundred longhorn*

up from Texas—couldn't been more than an hour—
Later, bold on sourmash, Ted asked how. *Strong legs,*
Johannsen slurred, *and split the brow when they lower*

their horns. He straddles the bars of the butcher rig,
clasping the guard with his thighs, while he swings the maul.

Nights like these, when trains idle three-deep in the yards

and drovers desert downed calves, they load every stall
five-full. Even from where Ted stands, scooping innards
and shit with a spade into holes, he hears the thuds,

the clatter of hoof against steel, the moan, the *scream*—
Ted pivots to see Johannsen slumped on the floor,
his purple thigh raveling like frayed hemp, then streams

of blood threading his fingers. Ted hits the buzzer
and runs, dragging Johannsen away from the pen
where the staggered steer froths and smashes his horn, hooked

on the bar, till it snaps and bleeds. When the cut-men
hoist him on the litter, Johannsen stutters, *I'm cooked.*
Once he's gone, each strikes the dead bull for fear or luck.

Letters from Eagle

> In 1897, Anna Malm emigrated from Finland to Eagle,
> Alaska, with her husband Abe to seek their fortune in the
> northern gold fields. Her business, Anna Malm's Arctic
> Laundry, supported Abe's prospecting for nearly fifteen
> years, before he died of cancer in 1913. At age seventy,
> Anna found herself alone in a mining village of fewer than
> one hundred people. To combat the solitude as that winter
> dragged into spring, she wrote daily letters to her sister in
> Finland.

Marie,
    I picked out this stationery
almost two years ago in Seattle
when Abe first took sick.
        The vines and berries

brought you to mind.

I've vowed to prattle
for a page each week to you, in hopes
of finding some quiet,

but now that I set
pen to paper, I have little of note
to report. Most is not news:

days get
warmer, filled with work, but nights the moon hangs
high overhead.

Other times, almost dawn,
the thawing river creaks like a spruce branch
sheathed with ice after a sudden spring storm.

Under the weight of such sorrow, could I break?

I'm tired and it's late.

Until next week.

*   *   *

Please forgive my excesses yesterday.

My mind has been overtaken by death
for too many years now.

I confess:
of late, I have begun to equate
the cancer that snaked through Abe's intestines
with the muddy men who crouch at my door.

I scrub out their clothes the same as before,
but I can't free myself of the notion
that they live underground, disappearing
like demons,

or worse, the creeping black death
that moles unseen through every living thing.

I can't sleep, wondering if, as I write

this letter, they're staking claim to my breath.

More nonsense, I know. Forgive me. Good night.

*   *   *

Marie,
      I woke this morning from a dream
I could neither shake nor fully recall,
so I set about my daily routine.

I melted the tallow from spare candles
along with two teaspoons of Abe's spiced rum.
By the time the day's trousers were blued and scrubbed,
the brew had reached a boil.
                I had to run
the pantlegs through the mangle, then rubbed
each crease with wax to hold the corners square.

As I watched my hands, the dream returned:

I was writing to you,
           today's letter,
but when my pen touched the page, the words blurred
and ran together.
         The image lingers
like ink clinging to my black-tipped fingers.

*   *   *

He died in his sleep.
         Just quit his breathing,
as if tired of it, and shuddered to show
his contempt. I sat at the bedside reading,
but he was gone before my book ever closed.

So I curled beside him to feel his heat.

The next day, the doctor came. He told me
Abe died peacefully, without pangs or grief,
and the preacher said this life's suffering
had reached its end.
                        But I say now to you,
that is when this life's suffering began.

What they call blessing has become my curse.

They didn't lie here with him, the night through,
feeling him turn stiff,
                        nor strip his soiled pants
and sheets,
                nor set them, that morning, to burn.

                *   *   *

I hope my silence has not worried you.

Since my last lines, two days have passed, I know,
but today the pale sky turned glacier blue
and cloudless—
                long enough the stubborn snow
issued fog.
                I wandered out, my shadow
still low, to gather washwater at noon.

You will think I'm indulging my sorrow,
but there is a living hush in our room,
a blood-pulse,
                like the inside of a tomb.

So I spent the day with a pick and yoke,

chopping ice from the water's edge, and stooped
like a pack-mule back home.
                         I'm stoking coals
and minding pails as I write these lines to you.

Cold steel beads. Drops roll down the way tears do.

      *   *   *

This is something I've never admitted.

All those years ago, when we reached the foot
of the mountain pass, Abe refused.
                         He gritted
his teeth and leaned near my face: *you do it,*
if you want it so much, but I'll ferry
no farther.
                    It weighs close to eighty pounds,
but more than that, the weight Abe could not carry
was the backbreaking burden of my doubt.
He felt bent and belittled by my lack
of faith, my fear his claims wouldn't pan out.

I strapped the washing machine to my back
and started up.
                         I see now that my doubt
was in every ironed shirt, each pair of pants.

Hung sheets greeted him with their jeering dance.

      *   *   *

Marie,
          Has sadness finally won my heart?
Please judge and tell me true:
                              the sun shone bright
today, the third day this week, so I hiked

down to the river to gather water.

When I arrived, I was staggered to find
the icejam had broken only minutes
before.
        Floes knocked and turned in the current.

I stood and watched the river start to glide,
and all at once, before I knew, I felt
the ghost-weight lift.
           There at the riverside,
I knelt in the snow and shook till I cried.

I vowed to write till I found some quiet.
I have—at least as much as one *can* find.
Be well.
      These vines and berries brought you to mind.

After an Unframed Original

Big Rock, Illinois, 1941

It must be August: grandma's cotton dress
summer-sheer and sun-dappled through the trees,

grandpa's shirtsleeves rolled over his brown arms.
His hands are calloused from years on the farm,

but he lifts his son like a delicate prize,
their only child, third born, first to survive.

We had to pace down rows, reading each stone,
in the wire-fenced churchyard at the edge of town,

before we found their weathered names. Breach births,
dad explained, forced out of the womb feet first.

I only heard grandma speak of them once,
how she felt her own body clamp her son's

until she smothered him, how her daughter
cried when the cord pulled tight around her.

Two years bent by the weight of their grief,
they hold this boy, their son, light as a leaf,

and won't tell him until he's old enough
to understand that like a lantern snuffed

too quick, the frail wick of what could have been
still burns in the dark rooms inside them.

In the distance, past their tiny garden,
a farmer and his mule team are starting

across the field, making a steady rut
for seed and rain. The furrow the doctor cut

across her stomach opened wide enough
for his pink body to rise like cicadas

in the cottonwoods singing themselves free
of their husks. If not for that, I wouldn't be

whispering this in your ear, a wonder
of happenstance that brings us together,

you stranger, dear friend, whoever-you-are,
this instant caught like a snapshot or scar.

The Slaughterhouse Wall

after Jerome Liebling

As if that whisper he sometimes thought he heard
over the constant howl of slaughter finally
tempted him away, his station stands deserted,

almost silent, without rattling gates, the volley
of shouts, bones cracking under the weight of his maul,
but behind where he stood, spatter-shot, caked with blood,

is an empty hourglass on the slaughterhouse wall.
As a boy, he made angels in the snow when clouds
pushed south from St. Paul, swinging his arms to record

the arc of his reach; now, even when he is gone,
his double, his shadow, has more cattle to knock.
His hand, though gone, leaves its blood negative, the palm

pressed briefly, against the streaked steel and cinderblock,
this once, a moment to catch his breath, a reprieve
before he leans out of the camera's frame

and into the world to come. Was this the life of
my grandfather, that stranger who gave me his name?
If I were ever asked, could I have done the same?

Beth Gylys (1964)

I initially began writing in form because I was determined to learn how to write a villanelle after initially trying to complete one and failing miserably. I finally managed to come up with a villanelle I liked, and it happened to be about a voyeur. My friend Dina Ben-Lev read the poem, liked it, and told me I should try to write a series of villanelles about sexual deviancies. I kind of took it as a challenge. I wrote something like forty villanelles in the course of a few months. One of the fun aspects of writing the villanelles was that I was regularly using fairly crass, sometimes graphic language and fitting it into this traditional French form that had been initially utilized in composing love poetry. I didn't think about it much when I was composing the sequence of villanelles mentioned, but I think my work did push against the boundaries of the form, because of the sexual subject matter and also because of the non-"poetic" language (for instance using fuck and luck as my two repeating end words in an initial tercet). Not all of the villanelles I composed were good—in fact, I only kept fourteen of them—but what happened to me during that intensive period of production is that I learned how form could stretch me—could make me use language in my poetry in ways that I hadn't ever done in free verse. Using form provided me a fresh new vehicle to ride during the creative process. I don't always write in form. In fact, I have been writing more in free verse over the last few years, but when a poem I'm working on isn't going anywhere, I regularly try to push it into form to see if that brings it to life.

The Trouble with Love Poems about Men

They're not of curves and shadows made.
They don't wear skirts to swoop and tease
the eye, nor toss their hair, nor sway.
So arduous to package men to please:
a slant of hip, or buttocks tucked in faded
jeans—they lack aesthetic flair. A spray

of curls might fan their brows, or bellies bloom
above their belts. To paint men in the best
of light requires certain skill. The groom

looks better if he's built. He'll fill
his tux with sculpted flesh. His chest
will taper to the cummerbund. Still,

what work to capture men's appeal!
A rise between the legs will also shade
and shape their usual lines. Alas, revealed,
the bulge is but a stick. We live dismayed.
It's difficult to bring men warm regard.
We try. Their love is always hard.

Marriage Song

Some have affairs. They never stop to think
until they're begging for a second chance.
(We love and learn we sometimes need a drink.)

Impatient with his life, he quipped, "We blink,
we're forty: with wives, kids, retirement plans."
Some have affairs. It isn't what they think.

He saw this woman at the skating rink,
watching their sons play hockey from the stands.
He fought the urge to ask her for a drink.

She wore those stretchy pants, a long faux mink,
slid next to him and said, "Hi, my name's Nance."
He wanted her right there. He couldn't think.

They fucked in hotel rooms, designer pink,
drank cheap champagne. He signed her underpants.
They fucked and ordered something else to drink.

His wife broke all the dishes in the sink,
took both the kids and flew first-class to France.
Some have affairs—it's never what they think.
We sigh and shake our heads. We have a drink.

Preference

Some people need a harsher kind of love.
I like the smooth soft wetness of our sex.
I like the gentle easy way we move,

our bodies blending in a fleshy weave,
our lips, torsos, tongues a sensuous mix.
Some people need a harsher kind of love.

One plays the master, the other plays the slave.
They plunge each other's depths with plastic dicks.
I like him gentle. I like his easy move

against me, desire rising like a wave
that draws us slowly to its crest then breaks.
Some women need a harsher kind of love.

A brutish forceful man is what they crave.
They scream and bite; they claw their lovers' backs.
I like the gentle, easy way you move,

and taste and touch my skin, without a glove,
or ropes to bind me. How could I relax,
confronted with a harsher kind of love?
I'll take the gentle, easy way we move.

Desire

Your penis fits quite fine between my thighs.
Come lie with me a while, this life is hell.
We're nothing but our bodies. Close your eyes

and let me touch you. I could see it rise
when I walked in. I'm not ashamed at all,

your penis fits so well between my thighs.

Why must we talk? I hate how words disguise.
I love the way we touch, and taste and smell,
reacting with our bodies. Close your eyes

and feel the truth of sex. It signifies
our wish to find the other side, a spell
the penis weaves between another's thighs,

the taste we have to beat the thing that dies
and bind the other to the self. We'll still
be bodies: naked limbs and hungry eyes.

We might desire the things that money buys,
but more we want to feel our soft hearts swell,
to take the penis warm between our thighs,
feel nothing but our bodies, close our eyes.

Adam Kirsch (1976)

For me, writing in form is not really a conscious decision, and certainly not a polemical statement. When a poem begins to take shape, the form and rhythm are present along with the subject; at any rate, I have often found that thinking of a subject is useless if the rhythm doesn't come with it. It is the tension between idea and form that seems to force the poem into being; both are equally important to whatever is driving towards expression.

Stepping back and considering the question critically, however, I can point to two related reasons why form appeals to me, as a principle and in the poetry I read. First, as Goethe wrote, "Working in constraints, the master reveals himself": only when there are rules can the game be played well. To force language to communicate despite arbitrary conventions is the goal of every writer, in prose no less than in verse; but in verse the conventions are more rigid, so that more resource and ingenuity are required. This is why only form offers that sense of perfection, of surprising rightness, that is one of the rarest pleasures of poetry.

At the same time, form compels the poet to shape experience into something measured, conventional, and public. This is an especially important point today, when the ideal of much poetry seems to be transcription—recording the motions of the mind or the vagaries of feeling as faithfully as possible. Even where this is done well, however, it is never very interesting; such poems remain tethered to the poet's private consciousness, instead of emerging into the public realm of art. Only a formed and limited object can be handed over, with artistic generosity, from writer to reader; only a shapely object stands a chance of surviving into the future. Using form is a token of the poet's desire, not just to commemorate, but to communicate.

Balsam

But look, there—who is that one, hurrying
Around the corner, swallowed by the crowd?
Already his face is vague—the only thing
I can remember is his voice, not loud,
His coat pulled tight around him, his head bowed,
As though he would have made himself so small

The world could not be sure that he was there at all.

Oh, but I know him! In this gentle street,
That sometimes seems too full of gentleness,
He tramples the gifts lying at his feet;
Wounded somehow, he feeds on his distress
And is not nourished. In his loneliness
He raises walls against the world that stands
Ready to take him up in its caressing hands.

City and night, and if there's anyone
Who watches us with love, do not forget
Him proud and helpless. When he's most alone,
And the city crowds around him desolate,
Lift up his downcast eyes; O Father, let
Your thirsty one know the redeeming taste
Of the thousand wells that stand around him in the waste.

Heroes Have the Whole Earth for Their Tomb

Tonight I read of an ancient war
Once thought self-evidently great,
Out-blazoning all that came before,
Each battlefield a hinge of fate,

And marvel once more at how the gain
Or loss of some extinguished city
Could cause defeated men such pain
And win for the conqueror such glory.

Who wondered then if Amphipolis
Merited agonizing death,
Or doubted that mighty Brasidas
Would, for as long as men drew breath,

Shine forth in his dear-bought renown?
And when did the majesty of act
Imperceptibly dwindle down
To indifferent, objective fact?

Athens and Sparta gripped each other
For thirty years; all those who died
Piled in a single trench together
Could not for an hour have pacified

Insatiable Passchendaele; the dead
Rise in an exponential series
From units in the Megarid
Up to the hundred thousand bodies

Now nourishing the green Ardennes.
If trophies were to be built for all,
The urns would leave no room for men,
The names would require an endless wall.

History that the Greeks released,
Unconscious of evil, from the lamp,
Now finds its scale so far increased
That atom-bomb and murder-camp

Draw less profusion from the heart
Than a few soldiers killed at sea
When Pericles, in the crowded mart,
Read out his invented eulogy.

Three Odes after Horace

I

Oh, Postumus, you crouch beneath
Your goodness as if it could be
A shield against senility,

82

The old-age home, blindness and death;

You brag about your discipline
Of kindness, prayer and sacrifice;
Do you think they will pay the price
The gods extort from living men?

Open your eyes! What saint or king
In all recorded history
Has been taken up bodily
To God, perched on an angel's wing?

Even if you're your body's slave—
You eat right, exercise, and sleep
With just one woman—you won't keep
Your precious self long from the grave.

No, you will leave your thriving firm,
Your wife, your car and house; not one
Of the shining projects you've begun
Will reach fruition then; the worm

Will suck your fat, while your accounts
Are drained to plump your worthy heir,
Who will be grateful you're not there
To scold as his expenses mount.

No, you will leave—and what you find
No honest man ventures to tell,
Except to guarantee it will
Be worse than what you left behind.

II

Now snow is abandoning the fields
    Before triumphant grass,
Now crumbling ice at the riverbank
    Allows the stream to pass—

As though there were a grace at play

In the seasons' constant round,
Or voices leading springtime on
   With low and lovely sound.

But "hopeless!" is their only word
   For men who stop to hear—
The days and hours are still at work
   To carry off the year;

And the moons that die from month to month
   Are reborn in the sky,
But you are an earthly thing, and fade
   Forever when you die.

Do you remember Orpheus
   Who thought he cheated death?
And have you heard of Lycaon,
   Begging to his last breath?

All that they had, genius and wealth
   And desperate eloquence
Was dust and shadow, faced with death's
   Placid indifference.

You do not own your days—tomorrow
   Is the gods' to give,
They who delight in teaching man
   He has no right to live;

And the snows that melt will fall again
   Upon this early grass—
Remember, and take up your life
   Before it too can pass.

III

See what I've done! No skyscraper or arch
Of triumph is bolder, or will last as long;
Pollution and vandals and incompetence

84

Will wreck those monuments; mine will survive.
I've beaten death; as long as there are men
Who bow and scrape to genius, I will find
Priests and disciples; even in that town
Where I grew up, they'll be force-fed my odes,
And know I made it out, to conquer Rome
And train the language into finer forms.
Muse, I have earned all this. Bring on your crown;
I'm waiting, and my head is lifted high.

Classic Crimes

Because he was foreign, young, and earned a wage,
She wrote hot letters and would have them dropped
Below his bedroom window; though she stopped
When a neighbor spoke of railroad-shares and marriage.
Now it was "dearest, wait a little while,"
And "you will have to teach me." But she knew
It had been "aren't you glad you let me do…?"
And other things, that came out at the trial.
To have run off with him would have been the grave,
But when she poisoned him they understood:
She chose being decent over being good,
The jurymen were flattered and forgave,
Since similar decencies had ruled their lives.
Such middle-class and law-affirming crimes
Grow sepia-toned, and serve to pass the time
Of prurient husbands and frustrated wives.

"The long, squat, leaden-windowed, burrow-like"

The long, squat, leaden-windowed, burrow-like
Offices terracing the Palisades
Seem the earliest architecture, such as make
On Afghan mountains bomb-proof barricades—
Or anywhere a Third World tenantry

Survives our televised annihilation
By clamping down and taking root. To see
On the Hudson echoes of such habitation
Once could provoke humility, the theme
For an abstract reverie that all is flux.
Staring across the river now, it seems
A sign of how civilization self-destructs:
Their single-minded virtuous contempt,
Our bashful Alexandrian tolerance,
Our glass towers and their common, huddling, cramped,
Impregnable cliffside. We don't stand a chance.

"Calmly, the papers calculate the chance"

Calmly, the papers calculate the chance
That in ten years the planet and a shard
Of rock will consummate the long romance
We've led with ruin. This will be ignored:
Not for the small but lotto-beating odds,
But from the madman's counterfactual ease
That fissions us as always into gods
Who count in aeons and eternities,
And beasts who scavenge for the daily kill,
Gobbling down the meat that will not keep.
Does the beast suspect that nuclear winter will
Be secretly welcome as untroubled sleep,
And does the god observe the sky in peace
Since his life neither starts or ends in weather?
Both let what will come come; for the decrees
Of the asteroid are righteous altogether.

April Lindner (1962)

For most of my writing life, I've been an unrepentant free verser, skeptical that rhyme and regular meter could capture the discord of contemporary America. As typical among any peers as that made me, a second tendency left me at odds with poetic fashion. Perhaps because both my parents were forced by the Great Depression to drop out of school, I've long been interested in writing approachably, producing poems that would yield meaning and give pleasure to even the most casual reader. Though skeptical at first of contemporary poets writing in form, I nonetheless found myself reading and rereading those poets we call New Formalists, in part because I recognized in them a certain clarity of vision, a transparency of expression, that wasn't unlike what I was trying for in my own work. As I read and reread formal poets, both of our age and the past, I found that the sounds—particularly of the iambic line—began to insinuate themselves into my ear, into my memory and poems. I would begin writing in free verse only to find iambs rising from the lines. It seemed many of my poems wanted to be written in iambics, and who was I to resist? Can a poet write clearly, for a general audience, in free verse? Certainly. Nevertheless, it seems to me that clarity of expression and regular meter have a natural affinity for each other. I'm interested both in exploiting that affinity and working against it, using received forms to speak clearly to the reader, even as I reach for the mysterious—the unsayable.

Girl

Plug her in, she's yours, twenty-four/seven,
the girl who glows and beckons from your screen.
Unfurling like a one-armed bandit's jackpot,
her body parts skirl past, bathed in blue light,
as lush as plums or cherries or split melon.
The airy tits of one girl float like clouds
above another's mega-legs, an ass
spliced from yet a third, these random fragments
assembled into woman by your eye,
real as a model airplane. If she speaks,
her come-on lines are scripted. If she's wrapped,

she's easy to unwrap; between her skin
and your parched lips nothing but convex glass.
Smiling is her job. She knows you want her
because who wouldn't? Hell, I want her too
or want to be her, sometimes, in the buzz
after I've stared too long, my flesh exhausted
by its own weight, my skin's dull tendency
to slough off into dust, the daily tug
toward obsolescence. I would hone my legs down—
they're all wrong—inject my lips with honey,
and paint my smile white as the Parthenon.
Beauty is truth, truth beauty—that is all?

No, beauty is the lie we'd carve and starve for.
We'd suck it till juice ran down our arms,
or live inside it like a suit of armor—
if only that were possible. Instead
we lie here, shipwrecked by her ceaseless motion.
Reaching for her prow, we catch her wake.

Crystal

It began as accident, a moment
beside you on a bench, our forearms touching.
(You didn't pull away; neither did I.)
As if our skins were porous and your soul
were liquid, you poured into me.
                                    Like crystal,
my voice took on a new note, full of you,
and from your voice I knew you likewise full,
our conversation vibrant as the chime
of champagne glasses touched in celebration,
a fragile music tuned by borrowed contents,
each narrow flute enriched by what it holds
the song provisional, the precise note
inspiring thirst, but altered by a sip.

The Rubin Vase

Suppose I say the hardest thing to say.
In a famous drawing two black silhouettes
gaze at each other, noses almost touching.
The viewer looks away, then glances back
and sees a different picture, a white chalice,
blank space between the faces seeping forward
to claim her eye. It's the profiles or the cup,
never both at once. The space between
two people—between us—can ebb or surge,
insistent as high tide seizing the shore.
Your fingers graze my skin, your body lowers
to press against my upward-arching body.
What I feel is that thin film of air
between our skins. These are the words that lurk
between the words I say. One day I can't
abide your touch; the next day I can't stand
its absence. Though the inner eye can't hold
two views at once, there's still the nagging sense
that with a blink the picture could change back.
Why should I say what echoes in my silence,
as if you've never seen the chasm between us,
as if, once seen, it could be overlooked.

Joshua Mehigan (1969)

One reason I began to write this way, trivial as it sounds, was jadedness. Eccentric practice seemed clichéd, I guess. Meter? Now, that was suitably outré! Pleasure has kept me hooked—the interplay of line and syntax, rhymes, accent and stress, really is (if the poem's a success) absorbing, and can take your breath away. Of course, from the perspective of a poet, meter and stanza forms, and patterned rhymes, offer some cognitive resistance, too. Rules of this nature stir up thought, or slow it, encourage industry, and oftentimes supply the means to show what skill can do.

The Optimist

The film showed stars of varying magnitude,
the right side Libra, and the left side Cancer,
mapping the brain's horizons, vanishing points
respectively of reason and desire.
The doctors liked her cheerful attitude,
hope being all she had in her position.

She waited, clam. Touch burned out first, then vision.
Emotion slipped. Last would be lungs and heart.
But, noting trends, they told her Taste was next.
She asked then, could they pick out her last dress?

She wasn't making light. It seemed to her
that cancer just rehearsed life's attitude
that one's desires must taper to a point,
which has position, but no magnitude.

Confusing Weather

The sun came to in late December. Spring
seemed just the thing that flattened into bloom
the murdered shrubs along the splintered fence.
The awnings sagged with puddles. Roads were streams.
Wet leaves in sheets streaked everything with rust.
The man who raked his lawn transferred a toad
too small to be a toad back to the woodpile.
In the countryside, he thought he spied the trust
that perished from his day to day relations.

His head was like a shoebox of old pictures,
each showing in the background, by some fluke,
its own catastrophe: divorce, lost friends,
a son whose number he could not recall—
this weather, nothing but a second fall,
ending, if somewhat late, just how fall ends.
Each day that week he sat outside awhile
and watched his shadow lengthen, disappear.
Then winter followed through its machinations,
crept up and snapped the green head off the year.

The Tyrant

When he came in before his wife, as always,
and hung his jacket on the hook, and sat,
and noted for the thousandth time the dull ways
that beams streamed through the panes and crawled the floor,
he recognized for once the light that strained
toward him. It was mercy. And the more
he tried to see it as a passing phase,
the more his marriage seemed to be just that:
a casual failure, not worth blame or praise,
but tolerance. Outside it gently rained—

a sun shower, something odd, an easy clue
that life's not merciless, but scatter-brained.
A rainbow circumscribed the joy he feigned
as the key turned; as she ducked past, withdrew.

The Murder

The man could tell this story by himself,
only love moved him past the terminus of voice.

He'd made a language out of adoration,
but then his mouth was too much dulling eloquence.

And then she left him sitting in a chair,
where his dumb fists fell in his lap like poisoned birds.

His choice became to die, or else to die.
His lack of choice became his life, and language left him.

But he had gestures just as good as words,
and, when he spoke again, he spoke with those. They said,

"The way to a woman's heart is through her chest."

War Dims Hopes for Peace

Nothing Will Be the Same in Land of Free
  Around the World, a Call for Faith and Prayers
Job 1 Must Be Return to Normalcy
  Bin Laden Praises God as World Despairs

Muslins Report Slurs, Threats, Obscenities
  Hundreds of Bomb Threats, Hoaxes Follow Violence
Bad News for US Civil Liberties
  Madonna Fans Observe a Moment's Silence

'All Necessary and Appropriate Force'
  More Rescue Workers Hurt as Search Turns Damp
Flight Schools Performed No Background Checks, Says Source
  It's Safety First as Yankees Open Camp

'Frasier' Creator Was 'Kind, Classy Man'
  One Hundred Ninety Dead at Pentagon
Evacuations in Afghanistan
  And, Valiantly, the Gruesome Work Goes On…

Joe Osterhaus (1960)

When I work on a poem, accentual syllabic meter and rhyme seem indispensable techniques for focusing my attention on phrasing, movement, music, tone. They are not, of course, the only formal means available. But for my purposes the ground notes of meter and rhyme, and the almost infinite variety possible within them, make them seem the most rewarding techniques.

The easiest answer to the question what attracted me to form is: Yeats, Frost, Thomas, Dickinson, Jonson. That attractiveness also has its roots in the to-the-quick completeness of my teachers' appreciation of metrical effects. And in the many hours I spent singing, in choirs and with a guitar, where the physical experience of fitting words to a measure made the attempt to write in meter seem natural, even inevitable.

Finally, in an interview Seamus Heaney characterized another effect of meter and rhyme that has been important to me as well: the back echo, the resonance or lift that continues after a line ends.

I do, however, feel impatient with the term "formalist," which seems so specific to our period. How is it that contemporary American poets who write in meter and rhyme are "formalists," while poets from earlier periods are not? Is Alexander Pope a "formalist"? William Blake? the early Robert Lowell? The strangeness of the term when yoked to such poets reveals its bias, even allowing for the differences created by their genius. Our use of the term seems to mean something like "a poet who chooses not to write in free verse," but when poets as different as Ransom and Crane can both be called "formalists," how useful is the term, finally?

Each poet is free to choose any technique, and to differ those techniques. My ideal readers will judge a poem by its phrasing, movement, music, tone; and will consider all technique, including meter and rhyme, as methods of achieving the qualities that make poetry such an essential art.

Dayr Amis

1

The buckling groundswells of the Middle East—
reprisals, strafings, heat, conscription, trade—
explained my mother's father to the last,
who, when still an adolescent, made

the trip he talked of in his final years
while standing at the counter in his shop.
In Dayr Amis, one of the village overseers
refused to back his horse even one step

in a blocked lane, and, always quick to use his fists,
my grandfather dragged him off and beat him in the square.
At home, he found his mother weeping, wrists
pressed to her eyes, for what he'd risked for her.

She knew that, if he stayed, he'd be locked up
and then conscripted to the Ottomans
to patrol the Bekka valley in a peaked cap.
So, hurried leave-takings: he rode at once

on a horse the family was rich enough to own
to Sidon, and bought passage on the docks;
a boy whose temper turned the green of vines
to gulls, corroded shadow, pulleys, locks.

He slept with others in the hold on straw,
his mind more on the barrels, hoops, and staves
so reminiscent of the monster's jaw
than on the gray horizon, or the sharp dip

of the slick deck as the ship rolled on the waves.
And though he never saw

his home again, its gardens knit a shape
that ruled our lives—millennial, green, roped, tiered,

they held a graded terrace, whose clear, sand-
bottomed pool reflected lemon trees and trained
our family toward what it might have had—
the whole a screen whose violation rayed

in sunburst faults, and branched in limbs where birds,
fresh-molted from shadow, darted, ruffled, shook.
Having sidestepped a soldier's cap and braids
he fed the gulls bobbing in the ship's wake;

a man who taught his daughter how to swim
by rowing her to the middle of a lake
where, in full sight of the houses on the shore,
he threw her from the boat, and, when she called him,

feathered the boat away with a single oar.

2

In my memory, he stands at the door
of his shop, unrolling the green awning;
indifferent to the light, as to the whir
the jointed handle made in the new morning.

Cigars, close shaves, the waxy bric-a-brac
he kept on the back shelves; each morning, he
took the first newspaper from off the stack
and read it as he bagged the Chinese tea,

black leaves crumbling on the thick-leaved foil.
This was the man we knew, an aproned clerk
who bartered with his customers, drained oil
into the street, and pressed us into work.

When as an infant I was first placed in his arms
he threw me in the air, as was the custom
in the old country. My father, shocked, pushed him
aside, and caught me as I dropped; in his alarm

dropping the Kodak and tripping its wire shutter.
The first shot thus a close-up of bleached grass,
the second shows him cradling me, oblivious
and smiling as the wind presses the wrap tighter.

3

Against the wishes of his family,
late in his life he bought a downtown lot
and tended it in his spare time; its tree
and gravel tasseled by his rake and bit.

Late one afternoon, he took me with him, as
he went to clear some brambles from the lot,
and, carrying a jar to hold the fireflies
I knew would start up from the saw-toothed grass

I struggled to keep up, so didn't notice when
the neighborhood gave way to scrapyards, lit
by fires still transparent in the sun.
And when we reached it; boundary traced out

by fence posts and wire, we set down our tools
and started, each according to his age.
I don't recall how long we worked, just that
when done we'd bared the many dead tree roots

smooth as the ribbed blond timbers of a stage.
In a few years, 'the college tapped the mint'
and bought his lot to build a new garage,
thus settling his short retirement.

When we finished, night was coming on;
the lot, though empty, tended, raked, and swept.
And as we tied the stripped branches with twine,
the capitol's white dome shone over the lot,

its shadowed ribs converging on a point
just broad enough for one; toward whose confine
the city, black streets and white marble, switched
its tunneling attention as it sought,

if not a 'witness, judge, or advocate,'
then some kind of intelligence for whom
the fires burning in abandoned lots
were part of a processional, in which

we too took part, as we walked back, carrying
yard tools and a meshed jar lit by fireflies.
If memory could occupy that height,
the moon would shift and radiate each street

until the empty downtown blazed with lights—
the sky's light, and the houses', and the banks'—
to stake a quarter that retained the night's
black warrens, but without the whistling spirit blanks

that haunted me as I walked back with him,
not knowing how to ask if he too felt that drone.
It spread like conscience through my breath and limbs,
and sealed me in a life he'd certainly disown.

Lake Endeavor
for Doug Tubbs

The night before a long-delayed, much-promised trip
my cousin and I carry shovels to a lot

where, in a black leaf pit fed by a crumbling stump
we heap, stir, and comb damp earth for the glistening rot

of night crawlers; blind flukes whose solitary trails
we pack and stand in breathing cartons on the porch.
At dawn, our fathers load them with our caps and reels
and drive us as we nod past stands of shivering birch

the color of the fishing line, until we see
the boxed-in lake, silvered by pleats of mist and glare.
Our fathers at the oars, we each kneel in the prow
and, rummaging the tacklebox for a hard orange lure,

push off, suspended on the lake's tympanic skin.
Our lines coil briefly on the water, settling in.

The Running of the Blues

Bronzed, haphazard sunbeams; a sky, cut through
by eye-flaws runneling from banks of cloud
toward the weak flints that trailed the receding waves;
we walked out far enough to watch the dunes'

inked hollows spread, and join, as evening
sprinkled opacity on the variegated water
like rust on the damaged grillwork of a car—
some fishermen ran past in twos and threes

and, dropping gear and tackle in the sand,
gazed into the sheared walls of the surf—
like a tray of spools bouncing down a stair
alewives were leaping from the breaking waves

and, straining forward, we too saw the streaks
of bluefish crowding toward the shore, to cut
the small fry off with the scimitar of air,
which grew electric with their dying: gulls

screaming as they wheeled down to pick off the few
leapt clear of the burst whitecaps and mist.
The fishermen in turn made short deft casts
and played out sagging lengths of line, until

the surging water snapped them taut; its weight
dragging at the checked reels, that ratcheted
and trilled in high short bursts. As one threw back
a too-small fish, you stepped closer, the wind

pressing your body through your rumpled dress,
and I felt your trembling as your still damp skin,
freckled with sand, flushed rough, smooth, warm; then slid
the moon from its wet pocket in the clouds.

As soon as their attack grew regular,
it stopped, and we turned back toward the pier, heavier
yet buoyed by the needling atmosphere;
the blue veins showing in our necks and wrists.

The shoreline neon staggering to life,
we slowed and watched a trident hook a blue,
the fish grinning and doffing a porkpie hat
as the tines withdrew; then walked on toward the pier

which ended with a burst view of the sky
but found the entrance boarded for the night.
Halting in the beautiful debris—
tiered cans in seaweed, polyps and glinting shells—

we chose a bar and sat down to a meal
pressed by the night drive still in front of us,
and argued pointlessly, and paid the bill,
and grew more awkward and too serious.

It was our shades who walked back to the car
and drove to Cambridge through the rising dew;
another shade who stayed to close the bar;
and, yes, a shade who says this now for you.

Alison Pelegrin (1972)

To the Reader:

Place, particularly Louisiana and the South, is of primary importance to me in
my work. In my mind, place and voice are closely connected, so it makes sense
for me to write dramatic monologues. The dramatic monologue also serves
nicely as a mask, and sometimes the easiest way to be honest is to hide. My
cast of characters includes Cajun and Zydeco musicians, as well as the people
who lived and worked around me on the Tickfaw River. I also have a woman
named LaDonna, and one named Eunice. And there are others. The people in
my poems are not spectacles; they are complicated and diverse. With all their
faults and quirks and moments of grace, they are like the working class people
who raised me.

As far as the technical matter of form is concerned, blank verse offers some
control over Louisiana dialect. I am also interested in the ballad, and forms that
have repeating lines, like the villanelle, have been especially welcome in my
poems about musicians. I also write in so-called free verse.

Never in my life have I picked up a pen and yellow tablet with the specific
intent of writing a sonnet or a villanelle or a free verse poem. When a poem is
happening in my mind the voice comes first. And when I hear people talking in
my head I write down what they say.

I'm Gonna Leave You, Chère

Woman, one morning
you'll open your eyes
and sweetest Pierre
will be gone—no goodbye.

I'll be in my pirogue
out at the spot
where I hooked the fattest
bass I ever caught.

I'll spend the day fishing
and drinking my beer
without ever wishing
I'd brung you out here.

Nighttime I'll dock
where the lake meets the river
and dance at Tin Lizzy's
and find a new lover.

I said I was going—
don't make the mistake
of thinking I'll listen
to excuses you make:

Pierre, Pierre,
don't leave today—
what about the fiddle
you love to play?

What about the hound dog
asleep in the yard?
Your children? Your house?
Is loving us so hard?

Pierre, come back, baby,
I'm losing my mind.
Who's going to warm
this pear of mine?

Don't lift your skirt up
and dance in your slip.
Don't try to kiss me
with your voodoo lips.

My dog doesn't love me—
you trained him to bark
at my fiddle and my footsteps

when I come home past dark.

And sex? You're pretending
or my name isn't Pierre—
I know what would happen
if I touched you down there.

I told you one morning
you'd open your eyes
to find sweet Pierre
had done left you. Goodbye.

The Summer of The Joy of Sex

My brother stripped Dad's dresser drawers
for smokes and found the book, spine split
to pages of arched bodies sexed and gleaming
beneath mirrors and grease.
Hey little sister—check it out.
We witnessed the slippery rub of cunnilingus
and poured over pictures of vulvas, each one blushed
deep red and shiny as waxed fruit.
We saw the penis and its bulbous cap, the anus
and its punctured grip, the flat slack paddles
of the breasts of a woman on her back.
A sudden distance stiffened like leagues between us.
From the winces in the pictures, we knew
we could only hurt ourselves or each other
with the accidental smash of our sexed parts.
But somehow we swam together, plunged
in full view on damp summer afternoons
beneath the heat of new rules:
No more heads dunked beneath the lucid blue spill
of the pool. No yanking my string bikini top.
No nipple flashing. No unanticipated touch.
We made these promises penis and vagina
wide-eyed different, hooked our crooked pinkies,
and fell back from the slick brick lip of the pool.

Bordelon's Blues

The Camaro won't start, the beer is warm
and far away the moon is cocked—a slug
bull's-eyed against the night. Bordelon is broke—
relighting cigarettes he's flicked into the yard,
wondering when he'll hook back up with work.
He's come to understand that life is small—
the smell of nicotine, his muscle car,
the woman smiling splinters at the bar
and the next day her kids calling after him
to stay. It always ends the same. He lights up,
promises to call, and walks away.
If she was pretty he might pat the dog.
Bordelon suffers through rotten dreams.
It doesn't matter where he sleeps—
the rain-gray mattress or the couch.
Every night is wasted if it doesn't bring
a woman in a bathing suit and heels
to lean across his spit-shined, won't-start car.
Without a woman near he'll drink and smoke
to sand the edges from his life and leave him
thinking every night's the same. He'll wake
ragged in yesterday's blue jeans, feel
on the floor for a shirt, and over Nescafe
pick riffs on his air guitar for people
he will never touch or see. Perhaps
they come from lives as small as his,
waking in the morning to count nickel change,
thinking of work and time off and money left
for a woman and a pack of smokes.

The Fiddle Player to His Love

Forget about the moon tonight,
leave the planets be.

It's our anniversary, chère,
seven years of you and me.

Times like this I want to overlook
all the nights you broke me up and left
me sleeping in my pick-up truck.
The way you bring a book to bed
and read the horoscope
with your sweet ass in my face.

I'll show you destiny—it's you and me
making history in the bedroom.
The tarot cards are telling you
to say my name, to scream so loud
the neighbors call the cops.

Cochon de lait,
I wish you'd leave astrology
and come sit with your sugar daddy.
Let me kneel on top of and play
a tune. Poof—you're covered in music.

Honey, you're the cookie
on top of Monkey Hill. Let me fill you up.
With only my fiddle to keep me warm,
I'm singing you a new song:
You got to let the salt meat in
to spice the pot. Heat up, little cabbage,
you're all I got.

Eunice Plays the Field: A Trenta-Sei

Romancing a plucker from Tyson,
doing a mechanic of the apocalypse,

any uncomfortable evening of not much fun—
this is Eunice's life, each blind date a trip
to a dimly-lit diner or parish fair;
all she can do is smile and pat her hair.

Doing a mechanic of the apocalypse
in the back of a souped-up Camaro—
that was the night she squeaked on the vinyl seats
and watched the green feelers on the clock glow.
She lost a pump somewhere on Algiers Point
after dinner at a lousy restaurant,

yet another evening of not much fun.
Her chest rumbles about love, too thankful
for men she ought to look at through a gun.
Once at Tipitina's a tourist pulled
her into dancing—she left early, alone
and with shoes in her hand, caught a cab home.

This is Eunice's life—each blind date a trip
to somewhere she didn't know she could get
to by car—cock fight and a kiss on the lips,
blood hen-pecked on the dress her best friend let
her borrow. The list goes on and on, almost
as dry as buttered slabs of Texas toast

in a dimly-lit diner. At the parish fair
her date spent an hour guessing her weight
in jellybeans and won her a stuffed bear
to prop between them in the Ferris wheel.
Of course her skirt flew up and caught her in the face
candy-coating the evening in total disgrace.

All she could do was smile and pat her hair,
hold in her tears until she shut the bedroom door.
At least she had on pretty underwear,
one luxury she makes herself afford.
Just in case she finds the perfect man
Eunice wears those frilly panties. She's got a plan.

The Zydeco Tablet

Who stole my monkey and my one good shoe?
I'm a traveling man looking for someone
To love at night, but every day I'm blue.

I'd walk ninety-five miles for a rendezvous,
Barefoot and bleeding, my collar undone.
Who stole my monkey and my one good shoe?

I'm the moody one coming to sing for you,
Rehearsing songs on my accordion.
I'm in love at night, but every day I'm blue.

I waltzed through Crowley in an orphan's suit,
No salt for the beans in my stew full of bones.
Who stole my monkey and one good shoe?

Cochon de lait, I'd swallow nails to look at you,
Say your name until my voice is gone.
I'm in love at night, but every day I'm blue.

Sugar, you're the morning star, the midnight moon.
Of all the ladies in the Delta you're the one
Who stole my monkey. You're one good shoe
To love at night, but every day I'm blue.

V. Penelope Pelizzon (1967)

Of Termites and Tetrameter

For years I've been returning to Lewis Thomas' *The Lives of a Cell*, toying
with his comparison between human languages and the collective work of
certain social insects. To paraphrase his observations, termites construct
prodigious dwelling mounds that can reach twenty feet in height. Individual
termites live only a month or so, yet colonies can expand the same mound for
sixty years or more. In its lifetime, then, a single termite will only build a tiny
portion of the whole. In fact, individual termites can't build anything; alone,
they scurry around aimlessly, swearing under their breath and dropping their
balls of mud. It's only when enough get together that some chemical language
tells them to pile their mudballs together and build up—and thus the arching
structure of the mound develops.

Like the tiny, short-lived termites in their colossal nests, individual humans
experience a fraction of their language's structure for a fraction of its existence.
Unlike the termites (we presume), we are more conscious of the labyrinthine
building we inhabit. And so during our lives—infinitesimal in relation to a
language's duration—we can play with the architecture.

Personally I've found experiences that forced me to confront the architecture
of English as influential to my writing as studying prosody. Functioning
for extended periods in another language—a language I still don't speak
well—brings everything heretofore natural about English words and syntax
into sharp relief as a construction, something so strikingly peculiar it might
have been built by bugs. (And the architectural metaphor comes home every
time I ask at a pensione in my childish Italian if I can have a stanza). For me,
it's necessary to lose English periodically in order to recognize the particular
shape of the rooms I inhabit.

Hours
            for Tony

Where were we bent, having trekked
all night from what place?
Now it escapes me. But *in medias res*,
                that baggage-checked,
between-trains, layover homelessness,
we found ourselves in Paris...*Paris!*

What *luxe et volupte* to wander
streets gemmed with market stalls
perfumed by a souks-worth of all
                comestible wonders
until, at the Jardin des Plantes, we wil-
ted onto a bench, to slowly unfurl

in the sun. Leaf negatives
swam through my lids, your shoulder
bolstered my cheek, passersby murmured
                fricatives
buffed smooth by the fountain's tumblers. No souvenir,
nothing to carry away but those hours.

Acqua Alta
            Venice, for A.C.

You shiver with the ague of all tourists who
                wash up in this mirror of water: every sight
        flickers, doubles, oozes an ormolu light
                    so locals, doing the same things locals do

        back home, look to you like Breathing Art.

They know what you are, and gracefully (or
            at least with pointed dignity) ignore
your feverishly-shuttering camera, wait to part

    the fool from her lire with candycolored glass,
            gelati, masks, or rides in gondolas.
You shoot the ladies playing tombola
            outside the church, the hopscotch-skipping class

            shrieking like they conceived the game. Each age
parades its idiosyncrasies, and though
            yours is a fin-de-siecle American ego
relying on a photograph to gauge

if it's "been there," try to disembark
            for once without a manufactured glance.
    Let your eye polish its *own* lens, whose essence
is water, whose films bear water's mark.

Songs for the Boisterous Month
            Anglo Saxon "Hlyd-Monath": March
    For K.H.

These dull, doggish,
cloud-drowned dawns,
the sluggard brain
drugs the body to lie abed;

my circadian chemical clockwork
waits, tickless,
for lighter fingers to wind it.

Till one morning in early March—
though each year I
forget the week, and wake
in shock—
all the birds are riotously back.

The eaves give shelter
and their wicker architecture starts.

After that, the receding hour
before light, *your* hour,
leads us by ear into summer.

. . .

The first to toss   its plum cockade to the wind's briskly
  martial riffle,   this violet's scent's so delicate
it can't be sensed   unless the thumbnail shako-plume's
ensconced in some   small vial that concentrates its smell
  (an odor scrawls   its signature illegibly
  till chemicals   made active by humidity
attach their cells   along receptors in your nose's
  epithelial   walls). A shot-glass makes a perfect
  biosphere,   distilling faint perfume into
  a mouth of air.   You take a swig of fizzing scent.
The sweetness stings   nervously along the chains
    to olfactory   synapses, and heats your insect
  brain, whose wings   all winter folded snug against
  the numbing cold   unfurl and *lo*—the insect sings.

. . .

A turncoat night brings winter back.
The crocus on the slope is glassed in ice.

. . .

The snows come down
        but do not stick to boughs that drip
        glassy pailletes from each tip.

A cardinal's flown
        from brambles where his startling cap
        prophecies their rising sap

across the lawn.
        Pecking flax from a feeder cup,
        he showers more than he picks up

till seed lies strewn
        below his swinging perch. His crop
        swells like a silk cravat. One hop—

he's gone.

...

The month's full moon at perigee:
its gravid luster limns each twig, so those
before its disk appear
a plexal web its weight hangs in.

First moon of the Roman calendar,
first born of the year.

New bark on her tongue,
the doe rests heavily in snow
and her buck lays down his horns.

Chelsea Rathburn (1975)

In school, I loved algebra and loathed geometry. I was attracted to proofs and theorems and being able to wiggle around the equations to solve for the unknown. Geometry, oddly enough, struck me as shapeless; I knew the answers were out there but I couldn't work them out. I suspect that the part of my brain that loved algebra is what draws me to formal poetry. Though I've heard others complain that form is constricting, I find the opposite is true. I have more fun with rhyme and meter, am forced to focus on the ways structure and content play against one another. I like knowing I must come up with multiple solutions. And I love how changing one word can shake an entire poem.

Because I truly do have fun working in meter and rhyme, I tend to write a few poems with a particular rhyme scheme or structure. I'm currently working on blank verse meditations, though I've taken up heroic couplets, quatrains with varying rhyme schemes, and so on, then set that form aside for a while. I'm playing around, basically. The form whose possibilities I don't think I will ever exhaust is the sonnet, which I believe is the perfect vehicle for compression and expression of ideas. I return to it again and again. In poetry and in life, I'm drawn to irony, the pull of opposing forces, the discrepancies between who we are and who we think we are, what we want and what we get. Form in poetry is itself a kind of irony—the preposterous suggestion that we can control the universe of a poem by imposing regularity. There's so little we can control, yet we keep trying. For me, formal verse has an elegance that both disguises and highlights the chaos that lies within.

Eurydice Alive

An ordinary girl the poet prized,
she was transformed by love-song from the start,
and when the viper's tooth wrenched them apart,
she was, through his long grief, immortalized.

And had she lived, would it have gone like this:
interminable evenings by the fire,
Orpheus on the godforsaken lyre

in praise of all the sweetness in her kiss?

She'd tell her friends she'd never asked for much,
but forced to listen to the standard news
of passion, love, etc., for his muse,
she'd grown to loathe the prospect of his touch

till hearing the thousandth tribute to her grace,
she'd notice how the subject of the song
is loveliest when mute. Would she then long
to slip into the venomous embrace?

Argument in a Restaurant

We've all seen it before:
the single, sudden shout,
her stumble toward the door,
his thick arm lurching out.

Not wanting to be rude,
we look down with a smirk,
returning to our food,
forgetting love takes work.

Then one day their fate's ours.
An innocent remark
mysteriously sours.
The chintzy, lightweight fork

a weapon in our hands,
the tears come. We begin
to stammer our demands.
No use. We never win.

And though we're circumspect,
our flaws shine on display.
The waitress brings the check,

the patrons look away.

We grab our coats and walk
shame-faced through the place.
Tables resume their talk,
don't meet our bleary gaze.

Yet when we reach the car,
expecting chill or violence,
we return to what we were,
and in the common silence,

the dark, receding danger
gives way to strange relief,
the flash of public anger
stilling the private grief.

Sixteen

After eight straight weeks of summer drought,
the tomatoes hang deflated in the yard;
even the weeds have flickered and gone out.
I water anyway, the lonely guard
of hard dry rows of beans, a burning lawn.
Inside, my daughter slinks—a perfumed sigh
and too-tight shorts. She shouts she's off, is gone
in a flash and a rubber squeal, no kiss goodbye.
For years she sat with me beneath the trees
and hunted bearded gnomes and four-leaf clover.
But that was when she still had knobby knees
and loved her mother. Those days are over.
Remembering April, the whole world wet and green,
I pray for rain, for seven, for seventeen.

Fireworks

Although we watched, the city's grand display
seemed still and tame, a galaxy away
from where we saw our sky explode with fire.
We'd always choose our smaller, private choir
of penny crackers, bombs bought for a quarter,
the rockets someone smuggled from the border
and lit out of the nosy neighbors' view.
With every year, it was the same and new,
the rituals of barbecue and soda,
the fights to light the grand Chinese pagoda
or be the one to spark the biggest flame.

At seven, nine, or twelve we couldn't name
just what it was that conjured their dark powers,
that held us hot and swatting bugs for hours
while howling sparks and flying discs of light
would chase our dads and threaten to ignite
the trees. Whatever it was, we understood
that grown-ups felt it too: in Hollywood,
the artful angling of the camera's eye
moved from a kiss up to a blazing sky
to show that love was powerful and grand
as the piles of Carolina contraband
that filled our yard. Like love, it may have been
the tantalizing risk that drew us in,
our traded tales of eyes blown out by glass,
a severed hand found hidden in the grass,
two fingers lost to slowness at the fuse.

We told of what we couldn't bear to lose
and knew that as we swore the truth, we lied,
convinced that our beloved China Bride,
the Taj Mahal, the flickering Hummingbird
were innocent, no matter what we heard.
And in the end, perhaps it was the names

that pulled us from our other summer games
and filled our dreams with dragons, light, and noise,
with porcelain China Dolls and Soldier Boys.

After the best explosions, no one spoke
but watched the avenue fill up with smoke,
standing in awe along the ashy walk.
Even the adults gave up their talk
of mortgages and financing our college
and set aside the awful, grown-up knowledge
of the natural law of diminishing returns
that marks our waking lives and all that burns.
We learned it soon enough: even the spark
which gave the loudest scream in purple dark,
would be reduced to nothing, once complete,
a little pile of litter in the street.

Unused Lines

While words we pamper and protect
march off in search of meager fame,
these lines like bastard kids collect,
skulking through our notes in shame,

the discards of our intellect,
false starts, limp rhymes, feet bruised and lame,
condemned to suffer in neglect,
half-breeds that we refuse to name

for fear they'll prove what we suspect:
the damned and saved are much the same.

Jennifer Reeser (1968)

My relationships with form are myriad and complex. First and foremost, I've always been a music lover—and (generally), the more ordered the music, the better: the choruses, the repeating motifs, the structured measures. I've always wanted to be a composer. There's an almost-unbearable beauty to be achieved through order. Music is the least tainted art we know, and the one I believe toward which all art strives: pure aesthetics, completely divorced from meaning, akin to numbers in its link between the "real" and the intangible. From my earliest days, the poetry of Shakespeare and Elizabeth Barrett Browning, for example, has given me profound pleasure in its harmonies and musical realizations, a pleasure I want to pass on, a tradition I cannot stand to see die. But in addition, I've found I benefit from the discipline of writing in form. It simultaneously provides me with poetic "water" when the well is dry, a manageable limit on my possibilities in expression, a jumping-off point for experimentation—something I do a great deal—and a not-insignificant comfort factor. Many of my earliest poems were, (as some still are), in free verse, but they suffered from bathos in the extreme. I discovered that concentrating on form alleviated some of the bathos. And in terms of assurance: I remember hearing a story about a group of schoolchildren—happy, confident and creative on their school playground, separated by a fence from nearby traffic and the chaos of the surrounding world. Once the fence was removed, however, the children grew more and more anxious without their protective boundary to give them freedom. I suppose in many ways, I am one of those schoolchildren.

The Centerfold

The night she phoned your father out of town
while you were dreaming in a suite of pink
and faithful things, you never heard the voice—
the sweet, high voice—answering her, instead.
"She meant much less than nothing," he would say,
and never hear your mother cry, the way
you would, between the atmospheres of rooms
she'd swept clean of his magazine mistresses
with you alongside, studying each one's

peak, seamless flesh and coyness-cum-aplomb
before you eased them in the garbage can,
to think, "And these are what I must become.
These are the venerations of a man;"
then hour by hour, witness the warmest source
of beauty in your world begin to chill
by neat degrees within your mother's face—
but see, above your bedroom windowsill,
reflections grown more beautiful each day.
Whose echo eyes were these, whose collarbone
so keenly hued and hung, whose mythic form
evinced in shades of glass against the pane?
Only those of a girl who now lay dreaming
in time she'd make each manhood testify,
"She meant much less than nothing," though she knew
she'd found the power to fold the words in two.

.

Not Even In Dreams

Not even in a dream did I allow
another love to lie here; even so,
why you prefer her mouth to my mouth now—
my mouth, that bears a scar from years ago—
should be no mystery to me. I never
expected to ensnare you with a smile,
though I expected something of forever.
It's dissipated to "a little while."
No, there's no pain, but neither is there sleep,
nor appetite. I'm tired by the dawn.
Simplicity's the company I keep
after the last of dusk is dead and gone.
And no, I have no penance to demand.
And yes, I've lost the faith to understand.

An Envelope For Jason

I woke up to the light of 3 A.M.,
your strong arms crossed around the pillowcase,
thick moonlight mirrored from your lovely face
beneath the window curtain's upraised hem,

where I'd forgotten once again to seal
out outer darkness from our bedroom dark.
The whiteness of your body carved a mark
like marble smoothed across the blanket teal.

With all my heart, I longed to photograph
you and that moment, but I was afraid
to stir or leave our sheets, and thus invade
such solemn sleep, and cut our love in half.

Why It Wasn't You

So tender were you in the love you made
to me, so slow against that chilly piece
of midnight—all the house at rest, afraid
to sigh or settle, lest your patience cease—
the walls themselves continued up, without
the slightest tremor at your gentle hand,
and no such fate as may squeeze faith from doubt
could hear those words you breathed, or understand.
So tender were you in your love to me,
but so inured was I to indiscretion,
outside, the rousing remnants of the sea
drowned out its cry, and I its soft confession,
even as your selfless body drowned the skin
that housed my heart, and whose love hid within.

'When I am dead, my dearest...'

The fear occasions me
that, having once been lost to you,
you wouldn't grieve—
someone with a waist and more constraint
acquired in less than sixty days, to sort
the swamp sunflower from black-eyed Susans,
and finally identify those violet, six-foot weeds
I love so well;

a fear you'd let the ground condemn my grave
to sentences of dandelions, or callous,
plastic lilies in some color I despise,
placed once, then left to topple south in fall;
it not mattering if you discovered (at long last)
a tolerance for bayous or the taste
of etouffée, but only that I hadn't
been the one persuading you; moreover,
you hadn't, in that hour, come to notice
mine wasn't the persuasion.

A.E. Stallings (1968)

The real question seems to me not "why use form" but "why NOT use form." Along with line-length, patterns of rime and meter are the only equipment a poet has that are not also in the toolbox of the prose writer; image, metaphor, synecdoche, anaphora, everything else—are common property. To make no use of these special tools whatsoever would seem an odd asceticism to me, especially since they bring such pleasure to the reader and to the writer.

As others have said, working with rime and meter can also be a way to tap into the subconscious. When you think to yourself, what rimes with x, you might be very surprised what pops into your head—it can be a kind of Rorschach test. It can also be a way of giving up the illusion of control you have while writing a poem. If you are writing a sonnet, some things are dictated to you—it is a way of mixing a little fate in with the free will (as I think Auden suggests somewhere)— some givens in with the variables that make for a mysterious algebra.

Meter and rime are not virtues in their own right, however. Poets should feel free to use them as they like without being matriculated into one "school" or another, or accused of betrayal or incompetence—to throw a rime in a free verse poem, to mix a short, emphatic line in among pentameters, or skipping anapests among iambs. Form is not dogma. To paraphrase T.S. Eliot, the real dichotomy isn't between formal and free, but between good and bad.

Explaining an Affinity for Bats

That they are only glimpsed in silhouette,
And seem something else at first—a swallow—
And move like new tunes, difficult to follow,
Staggering towards an obstacle they yet
Avoid in a last-minute pirouette,
Somehow telling solid things from hollow,
Sounding out how high a space, or shallow,
Revising into deepening violet.

That they sing—not the way the songbird sings

(Whose song is rote, to ornament, finesse)—
But travel by a sort of song that rings
True not in utterance, but harkenings,
Who find their way by calling into darkness
To hear their voice bounce off the shape of things.

The Charioteer
(Delphi Museum)

Lips apart, dry eyes steady,
He stands forever at the ready,

Fingers open, sensitive
To the horses' take and give

(Although no single steed remains
At the end of tangled reins).

It is as if we are not here—
The way the patient charioteer

Looks beyond us, into space,
For some sign to begin the race.

He has stared down centuries.
No wave from us, no sudden breeze,

Will trick him now to a false start.
He has learned the racer's art,

To stand watchful at the gate,
Empty out the mind, and wait.

As long as it is in our power
We gaze—maybe for half an hour—

Before we turn from him to go.
Outside, the hills begin to glow,

Burnished by a brazen sun
Whose course now is almost run.

We shiver, and around us feel
Vanished horses plunge and wheel.

Implements from the "Tomb of the Poet"
Piraeus Archeological Museum

On the journey to the mundane afterlife,
You travel equipped to carry on your trade:
A bronze, small-toothed saw to make repairs,
The stylus and the ink pot and the scraper,
Wax tablets bound into a little book.

Here is the tortoise shell for the cithara,
Bored through with holes for strings, natural sound box.
Here is the harp's wood triangle, all empty—
The sheep-gut having long since de-composed
Into a pure Pythagorean music.

The beeswax, frangible with centuries,
Has puzzled all your lyrics into silence.
I think you were a poet of perfection
Who fled still weighing one word with another,
Since wax forgives and warms beneath revision.

An Ancient Dog Grave, Unearthed During Construction of the Athens Metro

It is not the curled up bones, nor even the grave
That stops me, but the blue beads on the collar
(Whose leather has long gone the way of hides)—
The ones to ward off evil. A careful master
Even now protects a favorite, just so.
But what evil could she suffer after death?
I picture the loyal companion, bereaved of her master,
Trotting the long, dark way that slopes to the river,
Nearly trampled by all the nations marching down,
One war after another, flood or famine,
Her paws sucked by the thick, caliginous mud,
Deep as her dewclaws, near the river bank.
In the press for the ferry, who will lift her into the boat?
Will she cower under the pier and be forgotten,
Forever howling and whimpering, tail tucked under?
What stranger pays her passage? Perhaps she swims,
Dogpaddling the current of oblivion.
A shake as she scrambles ashore sets the beads jingling.
And then, that last, tense moment—touching noses
Once, twice, three times, with unleashed Cerberus.

Arrowhead Hunting

The land is full of what was lost. What's hidden
Rises to the surface after rain
In new-ploughed fields, and fields stubbled again:
The clay shards, foot and lip, that heaped the midden,

And here and there a blade or flakes of blade,
A patient art, knapped from a core of flint,
Most broken, few as coins new from the mint,
Perfect, shot through time as through a glade.

You cannot help but think how they were lost:

The quarry, fletched shaft in its flank, the blood
Whose trail soon vanished in the antlered wood,
Not just the meat, but what the weapon cost—

O hapless hunter, though your aim was true—
The spooked hart, wounded, fleeting in its fear—
And the sharpness honed with longing, year by year
Buried deeper, found someday, but not by you.

Thyme

I have some of it still,
We gathered on the hill,
In an empty glass, the bunch of wild thyme,

Faded now, and dried,
But in which yet abide
Some purple, a smell of summer in its prime,

When we stopped the car
Bought honey in a jar
At a roadside stand. It makes me think about

The theft of bloom, the sting,
A swiftness on the wing,
Things that sweetness cannot be without.

Minutes

Minutes swarm by, holding their dirty hands out,
Begging change, loose coins of your spare attention.
No one has the currency for them always;
Most go unnoticed.

Some are selling packets of paper tissues,
Some sell thyme they found growing wild on hillsides,
Some will offer shreds of accordion music,

Sad and nostalgic.

Some have only cards with implausible stories,
Badly spelled in rickety, limping letters,
"Help me—deaf, etcetera—one of seven
Brothers and sisters."

Others still accost the conspicuous lovers,
Plying flowers looted from cemeteries,
Buds already wilting, though filched from Tuesday's
Sumptuous funeral.

Who's to say which one of them finally snags you,
One you will remember from all that pass you,
One that makes you fish through your cluttered pockets,
Costing you something:

Maybe it's the girl with the funeral roses,
Five more left, her last, and you buy the whole lot,
Watching her run skipping away, work over,
Into the darkness;

Maybe it's the boy with the flute he fashioned
Out of plastic straws, and his strident singing,
Snatches from a melody in a language
No one can teach you.

Philip Stephens (1966)

A guy I knew told me I made a game of poetry by writing in rhyme and meter. He meant that rules make poetry frivolous. But frivolity lies mainly in content, not form. Besides, a game without rules is neither fun nor worth playing. Frost, riffing on Shakespeare, said, "play's the thing." How many meanings in that? Maneuver within limits, sure, but also perform music, make merry, tease, gamble, manipulate, act, etc. The thing? To say the least. I saw my first Shakespeare when I was twenty-five. *Romeo and Juliet.* Theater in the park. Muggy Kansas City. I'd been writing in rhyme and meter for some time, at first thinking I'd improve at free verse. I'd studied Shakespeare, sure, but that night I noticed for the first time tonal variations struck across a metered line, rhymes exploiting linkages between words, and twisted tales told in choice sentences. I started trying to put stories, entire novels, in blank verse and rhyming stanzas. Drama drove the meter, and meter drove the drama. Characters said one thing, but meant another. Ulteriority and irony thrive in a contained environment. Still, restrictions are a deceptive facet of the art. Poets draw on experience, emotion, skill, and the play of those who came before them to render strictures both moot *and* trenchant. This is hardly news or worthwhile polemic. Yes, Frost said writing free verse is playing tennis with the net down, and Sandburg countered that one could play better tennis with the net down. But compelling free verse is a game in which one finds lurking the ubiquitous iamb and other imperatives. Poetry is a little like golf. Or life. We play against ourselves and the course, and never get a perfect score. We can't quite win. But then, that isn't the thing, is it?

God Shed His Grace

I struggled to read Homer in translation
And keep my hands from trembling with the jolt
Of the commuter back to San Francisco.
I reeked of diesel smoke and creosote.
Sweat rings had stained the ankles of my boots.
Eleven hours and I would rise again
At four a.m., just barely able to make
A fist or hold a cup or grip a shovel.
The reading was a ruse. I craved no knowledge.

I wanted coffee, sleep, tobacco, supper,
And I'd grown tired of reading how that culture
Reveled in glories past and failures coming.
I dozed and woke, dozed. *The Iliad* fell.
I woke, head slick against the rattling pane,
And saw we'd passed Bay Meadows racetrack where
Retirees tottered on; they stunk of beer
And griped about their kids they never saw.
We'd passed Hillsdale; the pretty girls who worked
The shopping mall, offering up perfumes,
Sat still and straight in seats along the aisle.
We'd passed Bayshore; the Vietnamese man
Who each day wavered through the car, his workshirt
Gleaming with sweat and grease, his forearms bright
With metal filings from some tool and die,
Sat with his tiny daughter near the front.
He slept, his head swaying away and back
So that he sometimes brushed against her sleeve.
She didn't care. She stood up in her seat
And sang "America the Beautiful."
Two women back of me said she was *darling*
And *precious* and *an angel*. Storm clouds churned
Across the bay. All day our gang had watched
Them rise but roll no closer to the ditch
We dug by hand. But they came as again
She sang, "O beautiful for spacious skies,
For amber…For purple mountain majesties…
America, America, God shed…."
Maybe she sang it when her day began
After she'd pledged allegiance in her class.
Or maybe she was proud to learn it through
And sang it once again, not to forget.
One of the women shouted, "Look. Out there.
How the sun's shining on that cloud."

                                        "How lovely,"
The other said. "It's like the sky's on fire."
Then hard rain beat the thin walls of the train.
The girl sang louder, battling with the clatter

Of rain and wheels on tracks across the flat
That ran to Tunnel Three. Her father stood
And yelled at her, "Goddammit, you shut up.
I want to sleep. Shut up," and sat back down.
She sobbed and clutched the seat. We hit the tunnel,
Each rider's profile captured in the windows—
Retirees, pretty girls, and worn-out men,
The backs of heads like barley in a breeze.
But faintly, I could hear a woman humming.

Vineyard

"Six feet, huh?" Bodie Heller asked.
                              "That's right,"
My uncle said while we walked past bare vines
That clung to trellis wires like worn-out men.

"You measure if you want," the old man said.
"I know six feet." He swung his pick three times
Then paced the distance off and swung again.
We followed, digging clay, chucking stones,
And dropping spindly vines into the holes.

"You hear that whippoorwill up on your roof?"
I asked my uncle.
                        "Keep you awake?" he said.
"They will do that. They keep the bugs down, though."

"Up on your house?" said Bodie. "That's bad luck.
They say that whippoorwills are merciless souls
Crying for heaven. They say that souls get lost
And got to find things here to do."
                              "Bode drinks,"
My uncle whispered. "He's a worker, though."

"Six feet is how deep we dug graves at Dooley,"
Said Bodie. "That's hard work. It's rock and clay

And cold clear down."
                "This ground's not any good
For grapes or graves, huh Bode?" my uncle said.
"I dug my baby's grave," was Bodie's answer.
"You dig a baby's like a man's. Six feet.
My wife, she used to say I'd brought the dead
Back from the graveyard. Said they took the baby."

"You don't believe that stuff," my uncle said.
"Do you?"
           "Don't know. I know I didn't make
Enough to feed a baby. I know that line
Between the dead and living's awful thin.
You know the only way they know a man
Is dead is hold a mirror to his nose?"

"The only way?" my uncle said. "Come on."

A cardinal flitted through the tangled walls
Of cedar, oak, and ghosts of blooming dogwood.
What cheer, cheer, cheer, he cried. A bobwhite called.
"You hear?" the old man said. "He knows. *Bode's right,*
He says. *Bode's right.*" Bodie worked up his row
Until he stopped across from us and said,
"Years back, me and this old boy dug a plot
For some piss-poor dirt farmer name of Shipley.
This banker, name of Wills, comes down next day,
Says Shipley's in the wrong plot—Wills's plot.
We dig that coffin up, and when we do,
We see the seal's broke. Course, we have a look.
And there's old Shipley, eyes as wide as dollars,
Blue flesh, a twisted face. Got his hands
Up here, and every fingertip's scraped off.
Well, all Wills says is, 'Look like that old boy
Figured out he was in the wrong place too.'"

Bodie walked up the hill to get a shovel.
When he came back, he knelt and grabbed a vine.

"Looks dead," he said.
                    "It's not," my uncle said.
"It's green as grass."
                    "Just said it looked that way."
Then Bodie fished his pocketknife out, scored
The bark, and said, "Yessir." He dropped the vine
Into its hole then scraped and tamped the earth
With his bare hand. "Bode's right," he said. "Bode's right."

Hangman

Snow falls so hard the neighbors' windows seem
To stare at me through viscid cataracts,
And so I feel like I'm watched but unseen.
She's gone. The strokes took her away piecemeal:
Her reasoning failed, her left side lost all feeling,
But on the good days she'd ask where I was.
"Right here," I'd say. That answer didn't suit her,
So I'd ask her where I was: "Hunting quail,"
She'd say, or "playing poker," things I did
Before we married. Sometimes she'd mistake me
For suitors I'd contended with in school,
Or she'd hallucinate events from childhood:
A grassfire down the street, the shell-shocked soldier
Who swept the floor each night in Dunstan's Drugs,
Leeches she scraped barehanded from her shins
After she'd skinny-dipped in Francis Branch.
So quickly she regressed I thought of dolls
One twists apart to find another doll,
Another, and another, until what's left
Is nothing, the last piece lost some years ago.
Each day, though, I remain at my routine:
The morning paper's crossword, cups of coffee,
Then errands, supper, reading, and to bed.
But with this snow, the streets have disappeared.
It seems too soon for snow. I set out bowls
Of candy last night, like she always did,

But was disturbed when children rang the bell.
Swaddled in sheets, baring plastic fangs,
Laden with besoms, they cried *trick or treat*
As if the night were some uproarious joke.
It started snowing harder, and they vanished.
My neighbors turned their porch lights out, but still,
Teenagers from the run-down neighborhood
Just blocks from here kept knocking at the doors.
They wore jeans, hooded sweatshirts, and they stared
Through me unless I asked, "Where are your costumes?"
One of them always said: "These are our costumes."
This morning, thumbing to the crossword puzzle,
I read that in that neighborhood, a man
Fashioned a noose from an extension cord
Then climbed up in a tree in his front yard
And hanged himself. The corpse remained for days.
The neighbors thought it was a decoration,
Bound straw or newsprint dressed to scare the kids.
Without her, I've not finished many crosswords.
She'd putter in the kitchen while I called
For answers to the clues I couldn't get:
Eight letters, for example, river islands;
Or seven letters, pardon; or nine letters,
Ends with an *n*, a system of ID.
And thus, in turn, we'd fill the empty spaces,
Which is what pleased me, grids laid down like maps,
Lone letters as mysterious as runes,
Until each word or phrase we had to link
With ordinary human life was formed:
Sandbars or *amnesty* or *Bertillon*.
But I've been thinking of that children's game
Which takes two players. One knows the solution,
Draws lines for every letter of the phrase,
And then a bare-boned scaffold and a rope.
The other chooses letters that might fill
The blanks; however, with the first wrong choice
A circle's drawn below the rope, the next
Wrong choice, a line, and then more lines until

A human figure hangs, just as some nights
Like this, while snow erases all the streets,
A spindling dark form dangles from a branch—
A lower case *l* scratched inside a square,
Hinting at words like *life* or *loan* or *loss*.
No. It's an effigy in casual clothes
And at each gust, it kicks. What's it made of?
Old straw bound up with twine, the *Times*, the wind?

Ditch Digging

We—Hondo, Hawk, Smith, Sandoval, and Rome—
Stab with our picks and shovels at the loam,
The sand, black stones the size of hearts, then clay.
Layer by stubborn layer, we make our way
Half of a grave's depth down into the earth.
We sculpt a narrow ditch, for what it's worth,
And then we lay pipe, glue it, backfill in.
Next day, where that pipe stops, we start again.
And so on: pick and shovel, shovel, pick.
Steel blades thrust at the sticky grit go *tick*,
Chunk, tick, chunk, tick, the dreary, grating sound
Of rusted clock gears winding, finally, down.
If we were to look up we might observe
The main line, raw and quivering like a nerve,
The ganglia of spurs, the gleam of flies
Over a dead rat, piles of rotten ties,
Illegals by a boxcar boiling clothes,
Laborers stooping through the garlic rows,
And intermittent freight trains hurtling by
The cruciform poles stuck against the sky.
So we keep to the dirt and stony stacks
And kill the time by bitching about our backs,
The weather, foremen, union dues, or the jerk
Who drives by each day yelling *work, work*.
Spare those fanfares for the common grunts.
Ditch digging's just the shit work no one wants.

It isn't science, and it isn't art.
Quite senselessly, we pick some earth apart
And put it back, almost like before.
Nothing changes. Nothing. Nothing more
Except when day ends, Rome might tell a joke,
And we'll drink coffee, chew, or have a smoke,
Turning our backs on the little sinking scar
Of broken dirt that leads to where we are.

Everyman's Actor

"An everyman's actor," so the papers sighed,
Succumbed to injuries suffered from a fall
In L.A. on the same day Elvis died.
Therefore, the press his death received was small.

But from the obits printed we can glean
He had a "neighborly face," "a subtle skill
At showing slight emotion," and "a keen
Talent for slipping into roles at will

While often going unnoticed." So it goes,
If our own lives are any indication.
But our man had three-hundred TV shows
To his good credit, two still in syndication.

He played the coroner in Vertigo.
Or was it Rope? He was a favorite
Of Wilder. Or Ford. Or someone you should know.
And once he was a just-off-Broadway hit

In some rendition of that play by—Marlowe?—
Which called enough attention to his art
He dated Bette Davis. Or else Jean Harlow.
Or some fast-rising starlet who broke his heart,

Such as it was, or such as we can tell,
Which we cannot, for our man was an actor,
His body his instrument, a plastic shell
He blew lines through, his mind another factor

Entirely. Maybe he flashed that swimming star
During a pool party; that was one rumor.
He went on benders, yes, and crashed his car
In Oxnard, but still, he kept his sense of humor

Upon arrest. A man who made it through
The world all this world is, he milked his talents.
He played his part, made scenes, then took his cue.
Somehow up to the end he kept his balance,

While others took the credit, as their right.
Thus, in a recent cable retrospective
That dredged old character actors to the light,
His third wife out of four gave her perspective:

"He picked a lousy day to die," she said.
"He had bad timing, Christ, but he persisted.
He could be anyone. Now that he's dead,
I guess it's hard to tell that he existed."

Nativity

My church is old. We're getting on in years.
I swaddled up the nursery's plastic doll
Whose eyes when it was tilted squeezed out tears.
One eye looked rusted shut. One watched the wall
Farthest from us where shadows seemed to crawl
Behind the floodlit forms of one frail goat,
One bathrobed Joseph, one virgin in her coat.

My wife would cast a mob scene come December:
Innkeeper, angels, shepherds with sheep in place

Around a trough stocked with our newest member.
Brimstone and fire is fine, but give them grace,
She'd say. Show them God has a child's sweet face.
She's gone five years. Others too have passed.
And what I work with is a skeleton cast.

Mary was Susanne Bond. She learned ballet,
Then fled our fold to be a Vegas dancer.
Though some believe she lost the narrow way,
She came back when her mother died of cancer.
She asked my why. I didn't have an answer.
But Susanne sold her red Mercedes-Benz,
A gift from one of her old surgeon friends.

Joseph was Steven Lowe. He loved to sing.
In high school choir, his tenor stood alone.
Now he lays carpet, grouts tile. Late last spring,
While drunk, he broke his wife's left collarbone,
A sin for which he tried hard to atone.
After she took their son, Steve joined our choir
Of off-key voices quavering like plucked wire.

The goat was near to death, a mangy ram
On loan to us from Mrs. Samuel Newell—
Louise—who'd wanted to convert her Sam.
But he had work, his arm. Only a fool,
He'd say, loves a god so good at being cruel.
Louise spends every day at Brightside Care.
She pushes Sam around in his chrome chair.

But there my flock and I stood in the cold.
We stared as if some angel might bend near
The scattered straw or strum a harp of gold
Or tell us we had nothing left to fear.
Of course, a doll laid on a makeshift bier,
A goat, our newest members on their knees,
And a scrap-wood shed nailed between two trees

Was all we had to make of long ago
When love was born to save us from the dead,
Or from ourselves and what we come to know.
Myself, I watched the shadows. When Steven led
Us in a carol, though, I bowed my head,
Letting the others sing for the plastic child.
The living God. With whom I'm reconciled.

Diane Thiel (1967)

My strong interest in the many traditions of form has "informed" my attention to rhythm, sound, structure and other such concerns, even in my free verse. I am drawn to the possibilities form offers in terms of an undercurrent of lineage, a conversation with the past. There is a "ground beat" (to use Roethke's term) of tradition which I always listen for in poetry and strive to achieve in my own work. I naturally gravitate towards the musical possibilities of formal poetry.

Form also offers a kind of steadying in dealing with grief and hard truths. It can sometimes even help uncover these hard truths, because of the channeling and focus it provides. For example, the process of using the sonnet form for "At the Mailbox," with its closing couplet, pulled the true subject of the poem—how much one tolerates in life because one becomes accustomed—literally out of my subconscious. I am reminded of Seamus Heaney's reference to poetic form as both the "anchor and the ship," providing both a steadying and a buoyancy.

Rhyme and rhythm also offer opportunities for humor, and I've grown increasingly interested in exploring these possibilities, as in "Memento Mori in Middle School," "Bedside Readers," or "Editorial Suggestive," the latter being a conversation with Millay's poem, but in actuality, dealing with the issue of "editorial suggestives" I myself have received. I particularly appreciate humorous poetry, which has a serious underpinning.

Often, a poem begins revealing its shape in early drafts. For instance, in "Memento Mori in Middle School," the poem began truly emerging when it found its form as Dante's terza rima. The loose interpretation of terza rima (varying the end-rhymes: exact rhymes, slant rhymes, and assonance) seemed to best suit the conversational diction and tone of the poem. Though I have rarely used the sestina form, in "Love Letters," the oppressive nature of the described home discovered its poetic shape in the closed-in sestina. I have found that, given the repetitive nature of the form, many successful sestinas have a narrative charge about halfway through. In the case of "Love Letters," the father correcting the love letters adds momentum to the poem.

Music, humor, a sense of lineage, a steadying in dealing with difficult subjects, tapping into the subconscious —all of these are reasons I have such a close

relationship with form. Finding the form of each particular poem is an organic
process, which often incorporates all of these elements simultaneously.

Love Letters

My mother wanted to learn some German
for my father and because her children
could already speak it a little.
She was tired of dusting the stacks of books
she couldn't read, tired of the letters
she always had to ask him to translate.

He was usually willing to translate
the cards his mother had written in German.
But sometimes there were other letters,
and when he read them to her and the children,
she had the same feeling she'd had with books
before she learned to read, when she was little.

She said it bothered her a little
that her own children would have to translate
for her, that they could pick up the same books
that were as Greek to her as they were German.
She started learning it from her children
and decided to leave my father letters.

She wrote my father daily love letters
and carefully placed them on the little
table where they put things for the children,
next to our favorite set of translations
of fairy tales we first heard in German.
She leaned one every day against his books,

the white paper stark beside the dark books.
But my father never answered her letters.
Instead, he returned them with his German
corrections in the margin, his little

red marks—hieroglyphs for her to translate,
as if she were one of the children.

Maybe she was just one of the children
in that house surrounded by rows of books.
Maybe her whole life was a translation
of what she imagined in the letters.
The space between them made her that little
girl, wandering lost inside the German.

Because her own children were half-German,
she built her life around those little books
translating the lines of her own letters.

Memento Mori in Middle School

When I was twelve, I chose Dante's *Inferno*
in gifted class—an oral presentation
with visual aids. My brother, *il miglior fabbro*,

said he would draw the tortures. We used ten
red posterboards. That day, for school, I dressed
in pilgrim black, left earlier to hang them

around the class. The students were impressed.
The teacher, too. She acted quite amused
and peered too long at all the punishments.

We knew by reputation she was cruel.
The class could see a hint of twisted forms
and asked to be allowed to round the room

as I went through my final presentation.
We passed the first one, full of poets cut
out of special issue of *Horizon*.

The class thought these were such a boring set,
they probably deserved their tedious fates.
They liked the next, though—bodies blown about,

the lovers kept outside the tinfoil gates.
We had a new boy in our class named Paolo
and when I noted Paolo's wind-blown state

and pointed out Francesca, people howled.
I knew that more than one of us not-so-
covertly liked him. It seemed like hours

before we moved on to the gluttons, though,
where they could hold the cool fistfuls of slime
I brought from home. An extra touch. It sold

in canisters at toy stores at the time.
The students recognized the River Styx,
the logo of a favorite band of mine.

We moved downriver to the town of Dis,
which someone loudly re-named Dis and Dat.
And for the looming harpies and the furies,

who shrieked and tore things up, I had clipped out
the shrillest, most deserving teacher's heads
from our school paper, then thought better of it.

At the wood of suicides, we quieted.
Though no one in the room would say a word,
I know we couldn't help but think of Fred.

His name was in the news, though we had heard
he might have just been playing with the gun.
We moved on quickly by that huge, dark bird

and rode the flying monster, Geryon,
to reach the counselors, each wicked face,
again, I had resisted pasting in.

To represent the ice in that last place,
where Satan chewed the traitors' frozen heads,
my mother had insisted that I take

an ice-chest full of popsicles—to end
my gruesome project on a lighter note.
"It *is* a comedy, isn't it," she said.

She hadn't read the poem, or seen our art,
but asked me what had happened to the sweet,
angelic poems I once read and wrote.

The class, though, was delighted by the treat,
and at the last round, they all pushed to choose
their colors quickly, so they wouldn't melt.

The bell rang. Everyone ran out of school,
as always, yelling at the top of their lungs,
The *Inferno* fast forgotten, but their howls

showed off their darkened red and purple tongues.

Bedside Readers

Bukowski is not my favorite bedside read.
I've known one too many men who keep
a troubling volume tucked beside the bed,
in their apartments at the razor edge
of Terror Street and Agony Way,
where they keep Love, the dog from Hell, at bay
and let no daylight penetrate that lair.

And Larkin, there's another to beware
between the sheets, for all I like his form.
This be the verse to keep us all forewarned.
A life with Larkin would have made me dive

straight off that rocky coastal shelf—Believe
me this—unless you want a timely end,
Don't read your lover "Talking in Bed" in bed.

At the Mailbox

The first few times we met, our hearts would rise.
You must have thought that I had no excuse
since I am over a thousand times your size.
But ever since my brother introduced
the two of us, and showed his sibling love,
by catching you to put you in my hair—
I've had the kind that lizards can't get out of.
Now I tap the box to let you know I'm there,
a ritual we both appreciate.
Between my much awaited mail, you leave
your gifts. What would I do, if every day
my little house would open and receive
a mountain, where my living room once stood?
I'd move. At least, I like to think I would.

Echolocations

> *The waters compassed me about, even to the soul:*
> *the depth closed me round about,*
> *the weeds were wrapped about my head.*
> —Jonah 2:5

In *Boca Vieja*, on the unsettled stretch of beach
which formed the border between two continents,
a coast where water flowed down from the forest—
I had come to find the furthest distance.
At the end of a labyrinth of fallen boulders,
I came upon the massive skeleton,
the whitened frame reflecting back the sun.
The ribcage formed a passage to the sea,

where thin rivers ran between the bones,
dividing further as they reached the ocean.
The skull, half-buried in the sand, resembled
a house from some forgotten fairy tale.
I climbed in through the porthole of an eye,
looked out the double circles filled with light.

I found my way down what once her throat
and wandered through the gallery of bones.
Her ribcage framed the sea, the sky, the trees—
each canvas a vast range of blues and greens.
I reached the place that must have held her heart,
knowing, as a child, I could have fit inside
her vessels, even. I could have hidden there.
The tide was coming in, reclaiming things
clinging to the curved bones or roaming the shore—
the tiny hydroid forests with their medusae,
the limpets like small traveling volcanoes,
the scrolled whelks, drawing their maze of whorls,
only to be washed away. This was the end
of the whale's road. She passed her life to thousands.

I felt the sun-warm bone against my skin—
and a sudden heartbeat in the skeleton.
Her heart beat with a distant beckoning,
and in a moment I was with her, traveling
the *hwaelweg*, the road itself another kenning.
The ocean set the cadence, the swells singing
a line, receiving back another line—
in each reply, the slightest variation.
Our languages returning to the sounds
encoded in our strands, the spiral towers
of our helixes spinning round each other.
The calls reverberating through the waters
to navigate the depths, to guide us through
one ocean to another, the dark indigos,

the song returning from the deepest blues.

Editorial Suggestive (From a 21ˢᵗ Century Editor)

"What lips these lips have kissed and where and why"—
A hot beginning! What the readers want!
But could the lips be *hips* — get more "up front"
to better wake and shock the weary eye?
Must it be ghosts that tap the glass and sigh?
Why not a well-remembered lad at the front
door? (Or, better at the back?). You won't
quite let him in, but then—No, what have *I*
to say about it? It's your poem, n'est-ce
pas? *Lain*—Good verb—although the lay could be
more tempting. Set the reader's cheeks aflame.
Bend those boughs. Take him up against that tree—
out in that rain! And one more thing—oh, yes—
dear Edna, you must also change your name.

Daphne (A Photograph, 1930)

I know, in that moment caught, how she was fleeing—
her face eternally still, her body taut,
training every tendril of her being,
holding her in place—the raised knot

of her face eternally still, her body taught
by years of silence, that straight upper lip
holding her in place—the raised knot
of an old laurel tree, the tightening grip

of years of silence—that straight upper lip
we remember so much from the past. Poised, she stands
like an old laurel tree—the tightening grip
of that long summer falling like earth through her hands.

We remember so much from the past. Posed, she stands
by that field where she fell, her face in the hot grain
of that long summer, falling to Earth with her hands.
She would grind by stone and eat the seeds again

by that field where she fell, her face in the hot grain,
her mouth still. Closed. No one would see the swell
she would grind by stone—and eat the seeds again
that next Sunday at the cool garden table.

Her mouth still closed. No one would see the swell,
training every tendril of her being,
that next Sunday, at the cool garden table.
I know, in that moment caught, how she was fleeing.

Jennifer Tonge (1965)

One of my first poetry professors described form as the consolation of symmetry, and I suppose that's what draws me to it. I find myself using form most often in poems that involve emotional difficulty, even extremity, within or between individuals. In shaping the words on the page, I shape also the experience they relate, and that shaping, the tension between the words and the space around them, helps me to negotiate the territory through which I'm traveling. I find that I less often use set forms than I did when I was newer to writing poetry, but I often use forms of my own devising—idiosyncratic patterns of lines, for example, and patterns of internal rhyme. I also frequently use two-line and three-line stanzas. I compose on the computer screen, not on paper, because I have to see the shape of the poem as it's coming into being—I feel my way through the white space, as it were, and the constriction of that space forces the choices that make the poem. It's a sort of sculpting. In this way I'm constantly working in form.

Invitation

Each day I will go to the little garden
in front of Aya Sofya at 10:00 a.m.
with a Lonely Planet Travel Guide
and a pomegranate. If you don't come

between 10:00 and 10:30, I will leave;
I won't allow myself the cool reprieve
of that interior without you. After
one week I will stop waiting. I will leave

Istanbul for the extreme Northeast beyond
Trabzon, against the Georgian border, then on
to the isolate churches. I will swim
in the Black Sea. If, though, you respond,

we will enter Aya Sofya. I will lead

you among its columns and out beneath
its dome, and you will rise as I did, drawn
by your face into heaven. You will breathe

Aves—I tell you, that dome floats, for all
its actual stone, on the long last choral
note sung hundreds of years ago,
before the fall of Constantinople;

go up and touch it with your fingers—
an infinitesimal tremor lingers
there still. You will feel it on your skin
at the baths, a humming that rings

through the stone and light and water, in
the space between your skin and the hand
of the bathwoman. I will take you to the best
hamam; Catholic, you will feel the sin

of carnal pleasure as you are washed,
and maybe penance in the fine-ground pumice
that abrades your skin, the fierce rigor
with which you are kneaded. The little glass

of tea served at the end is a reward,
or a consolation. As you lean forward
to take it, say Ben de isterim—
I too want—and it will be proffered.

Tankas for Roxi

   Thai silk, iridescent,
lit, a peacock's spangled tail,
   and silver bangles
revolving on your wrists. They
made little chinks in your quiet

   room, where we spread quilts

and cushions on tatami.
　You gave me a turquoise
sarong to sleep in, and I shared
my ginger candy. Ting ting.

　It burned like copper
braziers on our tongues. You told
　stories like cinnabar
beads, carved and silk-strung.
You spoke of the dark rivers

　of Laos, and Kweilin's
tapered fingers, and a camp,
　where once a ghost came
to you, in search of a gift
that you, a skeptic, hadn't

　left outside your door.
You showed me bracelets chased
　with grinning dragons,
rings, and an odd stone lingam
that hung from your neck. I rubbed

　its sloped head with my thumb.
And there was a little purse,
　covered in tiny
cross-stitch and closed with a zip,
that you gave to me. Inside

　it was lined with dark
silk. I put my fingers in
　to feel it while you
poured me tea, talking about
each strange, exploding spice you'd

　tasted there. Songs trailed
longing from the tape-player,
　winding through your words,

and rain measured hours in basins
all over Taipei. Ghosts were

   being born in that
monsoon. They unfurled in smoke
   from the incense stick to limn
our skin and hair, came spinning
out between our words, and burst

   to silver paper
at the lamp. In its riddled
   light, we used our hands
to cast a shadow-play. They
darted, glanced, and parried

   while a subtle
alchemy of tense occurred.
   It flashed in our turns
of speech, freighted sentences
we never stopped to notice;

   we might have brushed it
with our finger-tips, but that
   was all. The moment
pulsed, as brief and gorgeous
as a tiger-lily.

   Then, in the stillness,
stippled by the second hand,
   the meridian opened
in the space that we had left,
and took us between its lips.

Acrostic at Sarah's Request

Exalt me into flesh, each nerve feathering
at your right touch. Odd cannibal, incarnate me in you.

Touch what's made expressly to be touched, tap as on a sugar

maple, when I say tongue, I mean that quick conjunction of flesh and flame-in excelsis-Deo, Deo,

The Mudanya Fig

If you would know me, you must break my skin—see, it's bruised
Nearly black with readiness. It will just tauten, then
Cleave and show my many constellations. Don't grimace;
Injury is part of every union. You want my
Ruddy pulp; you can't get it without using your teeth.

The Turkish Pear

A moment of renunciation—the world
Recedes beneath the sudden flush, gilt with lutes'
Minstrel notes. Each one flickers its tart edges,
Undone by that whispering sweet, the same sly
Tantalus that made you reach, that made you bite.

The Bursa Peach

See if you can do this cleanly: the cleft velvet
Envelopes—no, purses—unimaginable
Fullness; it will gush at your bite, it will drench you.
Think this hyperbole in what words you choose, staid
Adam reaching, then know it in the flesh: it is
Luscious beyond recall. But, you think, this region
Is famed also for its baths and its thick, thick towels

Peach

Come here's
a peach he said
    and held it out just far
enough to reach beyond his lap
    and off-

    ered me
a room the one
    room left he said in all
of Thessaloniki that night
    packed with

    traders
The peach was lush
    I hadn't slept for days
it was like velvet lips a lamp
    he smiled

    patted
the bed for me
    I knew it was in fact
the only room the only bed
    The peach

    trembled
and he said Come
    nodding to make me
agree I wanted the peach and
    the bed

    he said
to take it see
    how nice it was and I
thought how I could take it ginger-
    ly my

finger-
tips only touch-
   ing only it Not in
or out I stayed in the doorway
   watching

   a fly
He stroked the peach
   and asked where I was from
I said the States he smiled and asked
   how long

   I'd stay
The fly had found
   the peach I said I'd leave
for Turkey in the morning I
   wanted

   so much
to sleep and on
   a bed I thought of all
the ways to say that word
   and that

   they must
have gradient
   meanings He asked me did
I want the peach and I said sure
   and took

   it from
his hand He asked
   then if I'd take the room
It costs too much I said and turned
   to go

   He said

to stay a while
   and we could talk The sun
was going down I said no thanks
   I'd head

   out on
the late train but
   could I still have the peach
and what else could he say to that
   but yes

Catherine Tufariello (1963)

Writing in form was, at least in the beginning, not a conscious choice. From childhood on, most of the poems I loved and memorized—from Dr. Seuss and Mother Goose to Dickinson and Donne—were metrical and rhymed. When, at twelve or thirteen, I began writing my own verses, the lines that came first and determined the shape of the rest were metrical too; this seemed natural to me. Later on, I became aware that most people equated contemporary poetry with free verse, and that some of my teachers regarded my attachment to meter and rhyme as quaint and faintly embarrassing. In college I experimented a bit with free verse. But I didn't think much of the results, and the process lacked the sense of excitement and discovery I derived from working in form. A long dry period in my twenties, during which I pursued a Ph.D. in literature and wrote no poetry at all, was broken with a sonnet sequence. Since then, I haven't looked back.

Apart from the sheer pleasure that the pulse of meter and the sounds of rhyme afford me, perhaps the greatest benefit of form is that it forces me to push past my initial thoughts or impulses, past the first solutions that come to hand. It introduces an element of chance, of serendipity, into the process of writing a poem, and reveals to me things I didn't know I knew. Those who don't write in form often assume that meter and rhyme are constraints on imagination and expression. The commitment to a difficult form indeed forecloses most options, but at the same time it suggests other, less obvious possibilities that, without those constraints, might never have been perceived. I sometimes think of an elusive rhyme as Alice's White Rabbit: it can lead me into strange worlds far afield from where I began, and its pursuit has given me some of my best lines.

A related benefit of using form is that I feel able to address personal material more objectively than I otherwise could, with less danger of self-indulgence or solipsism. As Auden once wrote, "Blessed be all metrical rules that forbid automatic responses, / force us to have second thoughts, free from the fetters of Self." Form resists me the way the world does, and I love that resistance.

The Walrus at Coney Island

He lumbers into view at 2:15
Precisely, by a long-confirmed routine,
And barking hoarsely, slowly hoists himself
Into position on the rocky shelf
Where lunch is served—a shambling, bald, obese
Old man in slippers, knowing no release
Will come from jostling kids who crane and shriek
While harried parents smile. He's made to speak
For smelt and herring, which he gobbles whole
With comic slurps. His upturned face—the droll
Mustache and beard, the mournful bovine eyes—
Seem out of keeping with his giant size,
The dead, trapped power of the massive tail
Scraped audibly across the stone. The pail
Soon emptied, and the task of eating done,
His strength gives way: he crumples in the sun,
His skin an old tarpaulin's mottled brown.

Then, when the handler gives the order—*Down!*,—
And gestures to the pool, we catch our breath;
So perfectly he holds the pose of death,
We half-believe he'll never move again.
Once more the order's given. Only then
He stirs and lifts his head, heaving his wrecked
Resistant body wearily erect
And lunges as directed to the ledge,
Pausing to peer an instant from the edge.
All watchers gasp together as he dives,
The clumsy forefins clever now as knives,
The dark head bobbing in the dazzling spray
Of sun-shot water, like a child's at play.
So this is what he is, has always been:
A gleaming, sleekly muscled submarine,
Lithe as a dancer, roguish as a boy,
Corkscrewing downward with what looks like joy.

Elegy for Alice

I always assumed you were somewhere in the world,
And that someday we'd find each other again
And tell our adventures, like happy heroes
Reunited after years of wandering.

Hard to believe it's been a dozen years
Since we slogged together through the *Iliad*,
Longer than the whole of the Trojan War,
Or the wanderings of Odysseus afterward.

When your mother told me you were dead,
All I could think about was our favorite verb,
Μελλω, our rueful shorthand for regret,
To be about to do, but leave undone.

"I meant," you'd say, "to study Greek last night,"
And I'd reply, "I too, O Agathon,
Intended to accomplish many things
Before the light of rosy-fingered dawn."

And now it's seven years that you've been gone.
While I was living my ordinary life,
And carelessly, fondly imagining you in yours,
(Losing, in one of my many moves, the funny,

Wonderful letters you wrote me from Mexico),
I never dreamed that you would not grow old,
That time had stopped for you as suddenly
As for the daughters of weeping Hekabe

In burning Troy—the unremembered ones
You summoned from the ashes in the fall
Of 1983, when you were asked
To translate the catalogue of Priam's sons.

Hard to believe that you will not return
And tell your adventures in the other world,
No matter how tenderly I brush the dead
Leaves from your sleeping face, and call your name.

No Angel

All that thou sayest unto me I will do.
                                    Ruth 3:5

No angel stood there, only her mother-in-law,
Eyeing the bag of roasted grain and scheming,
Foretelling how she'd find him—sprawled and dreaming
Beside the barley sheaves, on bales of straw.
Like wings, she said, his cloak would cover them.
The plan risked everything. But as before—
While aisles of rustling wheatstalks whispered *Whore*—
Ruth walked alone through shuttered Bethlehem.

She stood above him. Started turning. Stayed.
The dozing reapers sighed but did not hear.
Watched by the neutral moon, she watched him stir,
Heard his stuttering snores, and was afraid.
A moment later, God did not appear,
And Boaz wakened to the scent of myrrh.

Rebekah

I used to listen to him while he prayed,
Wrapped in his father's mantle, for a son,
That God would grant me mercy. There was none.
How bitterly he must have felt betrayed

When ten years passed. Fifteen. Yet never cursed,
Though almost worse than anger was his look
Of baffled sorrow, as the bride he took

From God grew old. Meanwhile I burned with thirst

For him—the sweetness of his sweaty head,
His neck tasting of salt, our secret words,
His sturdy legs, his heartbeat like a bird's.
One night I woke and saw him by my bed—

He'd had a nightmare, and was crying. *There*,
I said, and reached for him. But he was made
Of shadows, and at once began to fade,
And at my touch he turned again to air.

But most nights, now, I lie awake and think,
Twisting the golden bracelet like a charm,
How I let down the pitcher on my arm
And spilled it in the stranger's hands to drink;

And when he'd had his fill, to his surprise
I ran back to the well. There was enough
For all ten camels, kneeling at the trough
With dusty necks, flicking away the flies.

I watch him sleep: no more a wife, a daughter,
Nothing but this one wish between the dry
Immensities of sand and empty sky,
My life contracted to a cry for water.

Fruitless

Now oleander flames along the beach
And tart green sea grapes ripen one by one,
While inland, warm and heavy in the sun,
The rosy mangoes dangle out of reach.
Alone these languid afternoons, I teach
Myself the names of trees. We're overrun
With litchi nuts, and then, their season done,
Pick sapodilla, sweet as any peach.

A mass of tangled green, the lawn's gone wild.
Another friend has had another child,
This one (she'd laughed, embarrassed) a surprise.
Small lizards, lithe in torrid silence, dart
Beneath beseeching sprays of bleeding heart
And blue and orange bird-of-paradise.

Useful Advice

You're 37? Don't you think that maybe
It's time you settled down and had a baby?

No wine? Does this mean happy news? I knew it!

Hey, are you sure you two know how to do it?

All Dennis has to do is look at me
And I'm knocked up.

         Some things aren't meant to be.
It's sad, but try to see this as God's will.

I've heard that sometimes when you take the Pill—

A friend of mine got pregnant when she stopped
Working so hard.

         Why don't you two adopt?
You'll have one of your own then, like my niece.

At work I heard about this herb from Greece—

My sister swears by *dong quai*. Want to try it?

Forget the high-tech stuff. Just change your diet.

It's true! Too much caffeine can make you sterile.

Yoga is good for that. My cousin Carol—

They have these ceremonies in Peru—

You mind my asking, is it him or you?

Have you tried acupuncture? Meditation?

It's in your head. Relax! Take a vacation
And have some fun. You think too much. Stop trying.

Did I say something wrong? Why are crying?

The Feast of the Tabernacles

After the final meal hurriedly eaten
Behind doors spattered with lambsblood, sandals and staff
Ready for flight, the rising dough in bowls
Brought on the journey unbaked, the wailing children
Snatched from sleep and huddled into clothes;
After the keening grief when the Egyptians
Found their own children smothered in their beds
Too suddenly for sound, and then the chase
Across the desert to the Sea of Reeds;
After plunging, panicked, through the corridor
Of water impossibly sundered like a chasm
On either side, then seeing the chariots
Of Pharaoh's army roll and disappear,
Shrieking horses and soldiers drowned alike
Under the crumpling walls: after all that,
They must have thought they saw the land of Canaan
Lushly shimmering in middle distance
Just beyond the column of white smoke—
Never that the high drama of departure

Would be followed by forty years of tedium,
More than fourteen thousand evening meals cooked
And eaten, pots scoured and clothing scrubbed
With never enough water, by stooping women,
While dust and sand got into everything.
Manna, glazing the ground the first morning
Of exile like flakes of hoarfrost, celestial food
Tasting of honey and coriander seed,
Soon grew monotonous as a steady diet.
For Moses, the exclusive interviews
On Sinai punctuated weary years
Of settling quarrels, hearing footsore stragglers
Ask again if they were almost there,
Or grumble resentfully that even bondage
Was better than a life of wandering.
Think how long it must have been before
The death of bitter nostalgia, then of desire
For a promised land that none would ever see;
Longer still before they welcomed joy
To the temporary shelter of the way,
Stars shining through the scattered branches.

Kevin Walzer (1968)

My initial training in poetry was in free-verse prosody, but after being exposed to traditional form in graduate school, I began increasingly to work in meter. I found that meter provided a useful "grid" to work from in structuring my lines, and therefore the flow of thought across those lines. By contrast, free verse required line-by-line decisions about structure; while this process can produce powerful poetry, it can also become a distraction because the poet has no framework to work within. Short-lined free verse produces one type of effect; longer lines produce very different effects.

As I became more comfortable with meter, I discovered that it offered as much potential for variety and invention as free verse, unlike what I had been taught as an undergraduate. I could work in a strict iambic line, for instance, or an accentual line if I wanted a jazzier rhythm. Rhyme added another, powerful dimension to my poetry unavailable in free verse. Different fixed forms, such as the villanelle and sonnet, offered yet further variety. Trying these different forms has allowed my poetry to deepen and diversify. Ultimately, traditional form—in its many varieties—is no straitjacket.

The Touch of Marriage

We touch, but cannot find our faces, here
in this new place.
                The bed isn't the same.
Our sides have switched, from left to right, and near
the window
              are only darkened woods;
                            the flame
of floodlights gone, the stranger dark plays tricks.
We try to kiss and nose bumps into chin.
We try again;
              our lips attempt to fix
on lips, but only graze the mouth. Within
this new dark,

we're truly in the dark.
But we are married here, and we persist;
eyes widen to find what little light
there is, and whispers trace us to lips;

we park
our lips together:

one kiss,

another kiss,
and then drift—

married touch replacing sight…

A Subjunctive Divorce

This empty apartment's silence could be mine
if I divorced my wife, or had never married.
The freedom of a bachelor would be fine
loneliness.

Silence would not be kind
even, if as a husband, I felt harried.
This empty apartment's silence could be mine
as its darkness is now. It's after nine,
my wife away.

After work, I tarried.
The freedom of a bachelor would be fine;
I could stay up all night, if so inclined,
or sleep twelve hours.

My whims would be varied.
This empty apartment's silence could be mine
forever,

if I were freed from marriage's binds.
My voice's empty echo would be buried
in the freedom

of a bachelor. Oh, how fine
such emptiness would be, like dust, refined
and untouched—a stillness

I find scary.
This empty apartment's silence could be mine.

Would
> the freedom of a bachelor be so fine?

Underwork

The owners had to sell, the neighbors smirked.
The strain. Divorce. Two kids.
> It's such a shame!
The bitter wife, the husband out of work.
But how can neighbors give this tale a name?
The truest signs
> are hidden from the street.
The story's shape is contoured by the house:
The bathroom needed work, and in the sheets,
they dreamed of a new jacuzzi,
> spouse and spouse.
Instead, the kids.
> The bathroom fix, they shirked.
The rotting bathroom floor let shafts of light
pierce up from down below,
> the underwork
decayed for years, and mostly
> out of sight.
When we moved in, we saw that floor was hollow,
thin, unsafe. Their marriage
> might have followed.

Before His Healing

for Dan

I.
The dew on the grass. The moistened earth.
The bodies nestled in zippered bags
are breathing. Above the soft dearth

of sound, an engine roars and drags
its pickup body across the farm
to where the sleeping children rest
in drunken calm. Today, what harm
can come to them? Now graduates,

their lives are free of rigid school.
One spins the truck across this space
to mark the day. He roars around
the field, tracks deep, the morning cool.
He does not see the covered face
his wheels will drive into the ground.

II.
The blinking message light. The words
are muffled in the tape recording:
"—a call from Mom and Dad. They heard
about him hurt from partying
at someone's farm, a party for grads—
there's not much information here.
I'll keep you posted, good or bad.
They're driving out there now." What fear

befalls them now: the briefest sketch
of what befalls a brother, a son.
Him hurt—this means a million things.
Their minds begin to whirl and wretch
from possibilities. Thoughts run
and fly and swoop on fearful wings.

III.
The chopper flew his body away
to rest in the hospital room, steel
now bolted into his scalp. The ways
a life can nearly go—the wheel
that ran across his head had snapped
the bones around his spine but not
the spine. So now his head is wrapped

with a cold steel circle, its slots

pinned by the bolts. A black halo.
Metaphor, no. Clinical, yes.
The halo locks the head and neck
to give the bones a chance to grow
and mend. He'll walk, they say. "God bless,"
they say, his living body wrecked.

IV.
He rests at home. The hospital bed
has followed him here and elevates
his monstrous gear: halo, head
shaved and stitched, reddened. Now late,
narcotically he breathes and sleeps,
the pain blunted by prescription.
His father sits. His mother weeps.
His brothers blanch at his description.

But still his body's healing there.
His neural fibers did not break,
shattered like a bridge in war.
His breath flows through his lungs; the air
carries his life. He'll soon awake.
His body knows what air is for.

Rachel Wetzsteon (1967)

I hope these four poems demonstrate my interest in marrying traditional forms and up-to-date subject matter. In "Love and Work" I use the ABBA quatrains of Tennyson's "In Memoriam" to describe what goes through a woman's mind as she prepares for a date; in "Little Song for a Big Night" I've stolen a stanza form invented by Louise Bogan; in "Madeleine for Awhile" I've used the Malaysian pantoum—a form involving elaborate repetition of lines—to try to mirror the vertiginous mood and theme of Hitchcock's movie; and in "Homage to Eddie Izzard" I've used the ghazal, a form consisting of couplets with a rhyme and refrain, to relate the experience of seeing this wonderfully wild comedian.

Love and Work

In an uncurtained room across the way
a woman in a tight dress paints her lips
a deeper red, and sizes up her hips
for signs of ounces gained since yesterday.

She has a thoughtful and a clever face,
but she is also smart enough to know
the truth: however large the brain may grow,
the lashes and the earrings must keep pace.

Although I've spread my books in front of me
with a majestic air of I'll show her,
I'm much less confident than I'd prefer,
and now I've started pacing nervously.

I'm poring over theorems, tomes and tracts.
I'm getting ready for a heavy date
by staying up ridiculously late.
But a small voice advises, Face the facts:

go on this way and you'll soon come to harm.
The world's most famous scholars wander down

the most appalling alleyways in town,
a blond and busty airhead on each arm.

There is an inner motor known as lust
that makes a man of learning walk a mile
to gratify his raging senses, while
the woman he can talk to gathers dust.

A chilling vision of the years ahead
invades my thoughts and widens like a stain:
a barren dance card and a teeming brain,
a crowded bookcase and an empty bed...

what if I compromised? I'd stay up late
to hone my elocutionary skills,
and at the crack of dawn I'd swallow pills
to calm my temper and control my weight,

but I just can't. Romantics, so far gone
they think their lovers live for wisdom, woo
by growing wiser; when I think of you
I find the nearest lamp and turn it on.

Great gods of longing, watch me as I work,
and if I sprout a martyr's smarmy grin
please find some violent way to do me in;
I'm burning all these candles not to shirk

a night of passion, but to give that night
a richly textured backdrop when it comes.
The girl who gets up from her desk and dumbs
her discourse down has never seen the flight

of wide-eyed starlings from their shabby cage;
the fool whose love is truest is the one
who knows a lover's work is never done.

I'll call you when I've finished one more page.

Little Song for a Big Night

What pure thought cannot contemplate
bent body understands;
why not kill time obeying its
crude, casual demands?
  Wake, limbs, wake
  beneath his knowing hands.

The conscience, high and mighty, says
all right, if you insist;
the convict, deeper down, records
the places he has kissed.
  Roll, parts, roll;
  make up for thrills you missed.

The harmless pleasure somehow leaves
a festering red sore;
the heart grows fond, the lust is just
as violent as before.
  Race, thoughts, race
  when healthy fun cries "More."

The body is nostalgic for
the dimple and the shin;
the soul is over in the wet wood
looking for its twin.
  Feel, fool, feel
  the double hell begin.

When one night hurries to a close

a residue remains;
romantics cannot separate
vast sighs from little stains.
  Sink, heart, sink
  into your last chains.

Madeline for Awhile

after Hitchcock's Vertigo

Scotty looked down from a very great height,
and as Midge sat primly at her easel
he talked himself back into wholeness:
"I look up, I look down, I look up, I look...."

As Midge sat primly at her easel
he followed Madeline through the city.
"I look up, I look down, I look up, I look...."
Down he fell all over again.

He followed Madeline through the city;
the ghost of mad Carlotta steered her.
Down he fell all over again:
she jumped in the water and he jumped after.

The ghost of mad Carlotta steered her:
"There's someone within me, and she says I must die."
She jumped in the water and he jumped after;
they kissed in the shade of ancient sequoias.

"There's someone within me, and she says I must die."
Haunted Madeline mounted the steps.
The kissed in the shade of ancient sequoias,
they parted when she leaped from the tower.

Haunted Madeline mounted the steps,
Scotty pursued, obsessed and dizzy.
They parted when she leaped from the tower,

they met again in a crowded rush hour.

Scotty pursued, obsessed and dizzy.
An ill-lit corridor led to her room.
They met again in a crowded rush hour;
they argued in her fleabag hotel.

An ill-lit corridor led to her room;
Judy's dark hair confused the picture.
They argued in her fleabag hotel.
"Be Madeline for awhile," he begged.

Judy's dark hair confused the picture,
ruining the marvelous story.
"Be Madeline for awhile," he begged,
so she returned a dazzling blonde.

Ruining the marvelous story,
her necklace revealed all she had been
when she returned a dazzling blonde.
Holding Madeline, he'd embraced air.

Her necklace revealed all she had been:
a stumble, a wail, a plunge into darkness.
Holding Madeline, he'd embraced air.
One final thing and he would be free.

A stumble, a wail, a plunge into darkness.
He talked himself back into wholeness:
one final thing and he would be free.
Scotty looked down from a very great height.

Homage to Eddie Izzard

What vision lights up wildernesses tonight?
The sentry scratches his head and guesses tonight.

Too many diplomas! Their frames cast gloomy shadows.
She flees the dark room and regresses tonight.

The cats are drilling for oil behind the sofa;
the stage fills up with rich excesses tonight.

He did a show in perfect French in Paris.
Qu'est-ce-que le mot juste pour *impresses* tonight?

The deity sounds strangely like James Mason,
for high and low exchange caresses tonight.

The shy commuters sit, lost in three-piece daydreams,
but this man practices what he professes tonight.

Bless me, father, for the man in makeup *moves* me,
the girl in the seventh row confesses tonight.

Do earwigs make chutney? Do spiders make gravy?
Is the hall enthralled by nonsense? Yes: his, tonight.

We'd grow too used to glamorous naysayers.
Only the final bow depresses tonight.

When I get home I'll place in the window
a candle lit for blokes in dresses tonight.

Sonny Williams (1967)

I look for that which is muscular, robust, and audible. I like poetry with attitude. I am drawn to humor and satire as well as to the somber. It seems foolish to ignore all the possibilities of sound and subject the tradition offers. Though I write in a number of forms, including "open" forms, I am particularly drawn to ballads, both literary and folk. Being from Texas, I enjoy listening to a number of Texas singer-songwriters who have composed blues and ballads, two forms that are intricately linked. Despite the literary establishment's general dismissal of ballads as cultural artifacts, artists like Lightnin' Hopkins, Townes Van Zandt, Guy Clark, and Robert Earl Keen have written fine ballads that have continued to draw large audiences, revealing the form's vitality.

My attraction to ballads is twofold; writing poetry and telling stories. The ballad is swift and compact; it is cinematic in effect with its "leaping and lingering," and the subject matter is as varied as the artist's own imagination. Charles Causley, in his introduction to *Modern Ballads and Story Poems* (1965), writes how the ballad allows the poet to speak "without bias or sentimentality" and "the incidents of his story to speak for themselves, and, as we listen, we remain watchful for all kinds of ironic understatements."

The Playboy

I, too, have lost many a girl,
Though still not shy to have a whirl
With one who might give me the eye
Or better yet, a rounded thigh:
Blue-eyed Anna played so coy,
Jenny dressed up like a boy,
Brown Larissa had thick lips,
Brightly colored fingertips,
Can't forget my dear Nadine,
Helped by tanning and saline,
Next Natasha stole my heart,
Red hair, her ass a work of art;
So all are gone and I'm alone
To count the loves that I have known,

184

But unlike Herrick, I won't die,
There's plenty other fish to fry.

Playing Basketball
for Rookie

When we were young, my brother and I would play
A dozen games of basketball behind
Our parent's house until the sun, a rind
Of slivered orange, had slowly slipped away.
And on our fence there grew a tangled mess
Of honeysuckle vines, nothing so nice
Or finely manicured as Dallas's
Japanese Garden with its pruned bonsai;

Those vines were wild, unruly, a heady scent
That sent our heads in dizzy motion like
A spinning ball, as summertime was spent
Rotating and releasing, movements that make
A faded sphere which sat against a clear
Blue sky a planet distant but familiar.

The Ballad of the Search Party

"Even in this world more things exist without our knowledge
than with it and the order in creation which you see is that which
you have put there, like a string in a maze, so that you will not lose
your way. For existence has its own order and that no man's mind
can compass, that mind itself being a fact among others."
                    —*Blood Meridian*, Cormac McCarthy

They tramped bootstrapped through grass with teeth,
with wooden faces through tussocks and sedge,
as apricot and blueberry grasshoppers
popped and sprang at the blackland's edge.

They searched in silence through upland savannahs,
through swales of bluestem and gumbo mud,
through grasses darkened by swelling dusk
as if they waded knee-deep in blood.

The air cut crisply across their cheeks
as the pandemonious sun froze
behind the shadow-folded hills,
and the sky deepened violet-blue,
layered pink as evening primrose.

They passed through crowds of wildflowers
that glimmered in the swelling moonlight
like tiny lanterns in half shadow,
bluebonnets, Indian paintbrush, black-eyed
Susans spread in a carpeted band,
then vanished in the darkened woodland.

The full white moon funneled the dark:
a telescopic tunnel of night
that narrowed to another world,
as if one could step into the circled light.

They followed the trail from the plateau
overlooking the oil-black river
into the moonlit canyon below,
through stands of ash and black willow

choked with underbrush, through brambles.
The sudden crack and snap of timber.
They hiked down into the cenote
where a waterfall muffled a distant coyote,
and the fleeting flutter of a golden-cheeked warbler.

They passed the lagoon, lima bean green
in daylight, that now gurgles in blackness,
the water-filled rim-stone pools like blood,
beneath the canopy of cypress,

a picture of the Pleistocene.

They walked beneath limestone marl,
draperies of travertine and dripstone
matted with maidenhair fern and orchids,
to the cave's mouth frozen agape
like a fossilized beast, a remnant bone.

They entered the dank and hollowed space,
flicked on their flashlights to some faded
script that was chalked upon the wall.
A quiet cough from the rank smell,
they ventured into the deepening gloom.

Circles of light trained their glow.
They crouched in that dreadful room
around the naked body of a child,
a frieze or a still life in chiaroscuro,
her neck sliced in a black smile,

blood dried and hardened to ceramic
on the stone floor, twisting in tendrils,
threading its way like tiny wine-dark rivers
until they stopped beside the rill.

They squatted, semi-erect, in that reek,
their faces half-lit like deformed death masks,
shadows swallowed everything else,
and nobody spoke, for no one could speak.

Death in Dallas

She died beside the piano
  She polished every day
On which, spread open like angel wings,
  Were hymns she could not play.

She thought it would bring some beauty.

She thought it would bring some class
To have an upright mahogany
  With pedals made of brass.

On it she placed a Bible,
  Photos of them all,
The flag from her father's funeral,
  In the front room down the hall.

She dreamed of all the music,
  Of a house that was filled with song,
Of little fingers tapping keys
  As Charlie sang along.

Her children have long since left.
  Her husband's a distant name.
"Beer!" he said in a booming voice,
  His eyes glued to the game.

He walked into the front room
  And saw her on the floor.
Silence drifted from wall to wall
  As it always had before.

He removed all of the photos,
  The Bible and flag packed away.
He sold the polished instrument
  With hymns no one could play.

Greg Williamson (1964)

I guess my metermaniacal tendencies are as much born as bred. So many ways to play the pipes, but I usually end up coming back to formal ones. It feels more natural, musically, thematically, for better or worse. And I like the sport of it, too, the wordsmanship. Monsieur Form sets up obstacles, then helps you dream up ways to get around them. That's just the way he is, no one knows why. There's a lot of mischief in his big heart. At one time, too, when police put out the APB, who wouldn't want to run with the likes of him, the artful little dodger. But that was then. And I like what John Ashbery says:

"These then were some hazards of the course,
Yet though we knew the course *was* hazards and nothing else
It was still a shock when, almost a quarter of a century later,
The clarity of the rules dawned on you for the first time.
They were the players, and we who had struggled at the game
Were merely spectators, though subject to its vicissitudes
And moving with it out of the tearful stadium, borne on shoulders, at last."

The hazards change with the course, but it's all hazards, and they're the players.
Nor does he say if it's in triumph or defeat you're borne out of the stadium,
        at last.

Origami

The kids are good at this. Their nimble fingers
Double and fold and double fold the pages,
Making mimetic icons for all ages.
The floor of the school is littered with dead ringers:

Songbirds that really flap their wings, rare cranes,
Bleached bonsai trees, pale ghouls, two kinds of hats,
Dwarf stars, white roses, Persian copycats,
Small packet boats, whole fleets of flyable planes.

Some of the girls, some of the older ones,
Make effigies of boys and…"Goodness sakes!"
They ask what I can make. "I make mistakes."
"No really, Mr. Greg!" They don't like puns.

I tear out a page and say, "I've made a bed."
They frown at me. I'll have to lie on it.
"See, it's a sheet." But they're not buying it,
And seem to imply ("you crazy!") it's all in my head.

I head for home, where even more white lies
Take shape. The page is a window filled with frost,
An unformed thought, a thought I had, but lost.
The page is the sclera of someone rolling his eyes

As it becomes (you'll recognize the trick)
Tomorrow morning, laundry on the line,
The South Pole, circa 1929,
The mainsail of the *Pequod*, Moby Dick,

The desert sand, the shore, the arctic waste
Of untold tales, where hero and author together
Must turn, out of the silence, into the whether-
Or-not-they-find-the-grail. Not to your taste?

The page is a flag of surrender. I surrender—
To the rustle of programs before a serious talk,
The sound of seashells, seas, the taste of chalk,
The ghost of snow, the ghost of the sky in December,

And frozen surfaces of ponds, which hide
Some frigid stirring, something. (What have I done?)
It's the napkin at a table set for one,
The shade drawn in a room where someone died.

The pages keep on turning. They assume
More shapes than I can put my finger on,
A wall of silence, curtains, doors, false dawn,

The stared-at ceiling of my rented room.

"You crazy, Mr. Greg." The voices call.
The sheet on the unmade bed is gone awry.
I sit at my little desk in mid-July
Throwing snowballs at the Sheetrock wall.

Double Exposures

1. Camera Shake with Wide-Angle
    Field of Snow

                Just got these photos back. Let's have a look.
Now what the—? Tell me it's not an overprint.
                I thought, you know, I'd stick 'em in a book,
But look at those warped trees, the aqua tint,
                "My Life in Pictures." Now I'm not so sure.
Its long horizon's tipping off the page.
                I mean, what *is* that red-eyed, furry blur?
Since "photos capture life," then by my gauge,
                It's either my own Henry Pussycat,
Turning upon the blue, inclining snow,
                Or Yeti. Hmm. You'd think I'd remember that.
The world's a whole lot weirder than we know.

The Muse Addresses the Poet
(and getteth alle up in hys face)

Just where do you get off, pal? Whoop-de-doo,
You found out words are fickle, that they lie
Right to your face. You boob, of course they do.
The first thing language did was ramify
Into a wandering wood as old as I
Am. Spenser scooped you. What's more, in a word

My good friend Harry Bailey might supply,
"Thy drasty rhyming is nat worth a toord."

Where'd I go wrong? Why do you still imbue
Creeks, flowers, leaves, moons, clouds, the whole dang sky
With hints of you? Even the old scops knew
That's unbacked specie, scrip that couldn't buy
The paper it's printed on, and as you tie
Some arbitrary value to a bird,
I'm not sure how to put this, but I'll try,
"Thy drasty rhyming is nat worth a toord."

Where was I? Oh, right. Lookit here, we're through
If you don't ditch that cluck you glorify,
Who's bored us all for aeons with his mew,
His pangs and inconveniences, the high
Regard for what he calls "My Self" (my eye!),
That tedious biography…! I've heard
All I can stomach of him, and by the by,
"Thy drasty rhyming is nat worth a toord."

The self-love. The sincerity! The sigh.
I've heard it all before. You're such a nerd.
Now tell your book to git. *Envoi.* Goodbye.
"Thy drasty rhyming is nat worth a toord."

The Life and Times of Wile E. Coyote, Super Genius

> *I am a genius by trade.*
> W. E. Coyote

With you afling, afang, not yet nonplussed,
Nemesis Roadrunner, Swift-footed, Taker-of-three-
Forks, strange kinetic fellow, animated
Character, that pluméd cuckoo, Bird

Thou never wert, sticks out his tongue, waves, peels
Out, and you wrap up a pileated
Bust of smoke. And now? What now? "I must
Dream up a *bril*liant master strategy,

In*ge*nious, *da*ring." Here's to you, Coyote.
Here's to Giant Fly Traps, Quick-Dry Cements,
To ACME Robots, glues, kites, keyhole saws,
DO-IT-YOURSELF TORNADOS, female bird
Impersonations, anvils, Earthquake Pills,...
And to the selective repeal of natural laws,
Schemus Backfiribus, a reverse Quixote:
Art turns to mere truth, what it represents,

Then, proven to be true, it turns fictitious.
Roadrunner goes right over the painted span,
You fall to the canyon floor, and from the phony
Tunnel comes the train, *engineered by the bird*,
Your foison, fantasy, feather in your cap,
The better life, your failure—like my own.
Wile. E. Everyman. Come, Trickster, let us
Feast on our clay chicken, our tin can.

Christian Wiman (1966)

I've written in unpunctuated free verse, rhymed free verse, strict metrical forms, invented forms using meter and rhyme, even prose poems. It seems to me as silly and self-defeating to forego some of the gains made by the Modernists and later poets as it is to eradicate the elements poetry has employed for thousands of years. You use what works, what the occasion calls for. That said, I am more drawn to poetry of contained formal expressiveness, a tight aural coherence of line and sound, even when a poem is in free verse (and perhaps especially then). Writing in traditional forms has been a natural extension of this preference, though I've never set out to write a sonnet or villanelle or what have you. The poem determines the form, always. No doubt at some level I *am* determining this, or the strengths and limitations of my temperament, talent, and reading are determining it. But I'm not altogether conscious of why certain occasions and feelings seem to need these forms, nor do I want to be.

A Field in Scurry County

Late evening, cool, September, the ground
giving its clays and contours to the sky.
The colors swirl and merge and fall back down
and for a moment, as the reds intensify,

I am a ghost of all I don't remember,
a grown man standing where a child once stood.
It is late evening. It is cool. September.
Pain like a breeze goes through me as if it could.

Rhymes for a Watertower

A town so flat a grave's a hill,
    A dusk the color of beer.
A row of schooldesks shadows fill,
    A row of houses near.

A courthouse spreading to its lawn,
    A bank clock's lingering heat.
A gleam of storefronts not quite gone,
    A courthouse in the street.

A different element, almost,
    A dry creek brimming black.
A light to lure the darkness close,
    A light to keep it back.

A time so still a heart's a sound,
    A moon the color of skin.
A pumpjack bowing to the ground,
    Again, again, again.

Poŝtolka
        (Prague)

When I was learning words
and you were in the bath
there was a flurry of small birds
and in the aftermath

of all that panicked flight,
as if the red dusk willed
a concentration of its light:
a falcon on the sill.

It scanned the orchard's bowers,
then pane by pane it eyed
the stories facing ours
but never looked inside.

I called you in to see.
And when you steamed the room
and naked next to me
stood dripping, as a bloom

of blood formed in your cheek
and slowly seemed to melt,
I could almost speak
the love I almost felt.

Wish for something, you said.
A shiver pricked your spine.
The falcon turned its head
and locked its eyes on mine.

For a long moment I'm still in
I wished and wished and wished
the moment would not end.
And just like that it vanished.

Sleeping in the Open

The touch that for one moment seemed
Her touch recovered in his dream

Is as he wakes only the wind
Moving over his bare skin

And through the single towering tree
That seems to rouse, seems a body

Responding and subsiding now
As if the years had taught it how

To be both taken and to stay
By giving inward and away

Whenever stirred by a real wind.
Even the strongest of them end.

Old Song, Long Night

If in some night of which I'm now a part
You wake in fear of nothing you can name
And, as you ease from loved ones, feel your heart
Quickening through your body with the same

Obscure imperative that I once knew,
Reading perhaps the very things I read
In search of something that will comfort you,
Some evidence that once the quickened dead

Endured a darkness that seemed all their own
And steeled themselves to name and feel each fear,
Then with each moment you are more alone,
More anxious, more afraid there's nothing here

But rage to sing some peace they'd never be,
Which dawns upon you as it dawned on me.

Hard Night

What words or harder gift
does the light require of me
carving from the dark
this difficult tree?

What place or farther peace
do I almost see
emerging from the night
and heart of me?

The sky whitens, goes on and on.
Fields wrinkle into rows
of cotton, go on and on.
Night like a fling of crows
disperses and is gone.

What song, what home,
what calm or one clarity
can I not quite come to,
never quite see:

this field, this sky, this tree.

Chryss Yost (1966)

Growing up in the 70's, my teachers ooohed and awwwed over my simple poems, which often included lines like "The leaves weep onto the sidewalk." My teachers were so impressed, or so busy cultivating my self-esteem, that they treated me like a master poet while I was still in elementary school. It was too easy. I grew bored with writing poetry and stopped writing it. It took me twenty years to discover there is more to the craft of poetry than weeping leaves, when John Ridland introduced me to form. I love form because it seems more playful than free verse, more likely to surprise the reader. Making a pattern, changing the pattern. It's like playing peek-a-boo with a child: covered face, uncovered face, covered face. Even a baby figures out the pattern pretty quickly. But then, if you stick out your tongue and roll your eyes when the kid is expecting a gentle smile, you're rewarded with giggles. Or tears. If you don't know what to expect, how can you be surprised? Delighted? Shocked? Of course, many free verse poems deliver a strong emotional punch, but I'm rarely moved at that immediate, reflexive level that comes from a good game of peek-a-boo.

Right now, I'm playing a lot with different ways of getting my poems to "click shut," and nothing seems to work as well as rhyme and meter. Writing poetry is the way I relax and have fun, so my desires as a poet may be different than those of someone writing as therapy, academic exercise, or political expression. I've been fortunate enough to meet some wonderful and supportive poets like Barry Spacks, John Ridland, Dana Gioia, and the West Chester Conference group. After all, if poetry is a game, it's more fun to play with friends.

Terzanelle in Blonde

Some things can be changed. Not yesterday
And not your leaving me. I'll dye my hair.
This blonde is too much yours for me today:

Too long and sentimental, unaware.
The insistent "if" of blonde, and "then,"
And not "you're leaving me." I'll dye my hair,

Until it's black as yours, and then again.
I'll dye until it's red or grey, to drown
The insistent "if" of blonde, and then

Your words becoming tied to hers, the sound
Of lovers' voices. Should be mine with yours.
I'll dye until it's red or grey, to drown

The echo of your whispers on my shoulders,
Saturate the swish of my own heart,
Of lovers' voices. Should be mine with yours

Tangled up for days, not torn apart.
Some things can be changed. Not yesterday,
Not your leaving, not the hardest part.
This blonde is too much yours for me today.

Lai with Sounds of Skin

Shall we dress in skin,
our living linen?
Bone weft,
pull of masculine
into feminine,
the heft,
the warp, the weave and spin
of carded days in

tightly-twisted thin
yarns that we begin—
like wool
like *will*, like *has been*,
spoken to silken—
to spool:
thick bolts of linen,
skin to skein to skin.

Advice for Women

Keep focused on the ceiling and you might
not bite your cheek too hard at the trespass
of cold metal sliding in. And you're right
to feel so pale and exposed (no mas-
ter of your body now!) Clinical light
keeps you composed here, but beyond the glass

window, in the lab next door, a glass
dish cultivates the worst in you. You might
give up the God you heard about in Mass
for antioxidants. There's time to right
your wrongs, and settle scores, before you pass
like breath remade as clouds by winter light

in sharp still mornings. Fluorescent light
rains down on you like blue-white sun in glass
test tubes, like luminescent dynamite.
The gossiping of cells is like a mass
of schoolgirls, watching in the hallway, right
before you stumble. Make small talk to pass

the time. Forget the test, of course you'll pass.
They look for microscopic faults with light
that radiates right through the you on glass.
They'll set aside the parts of you that might
grow into something more. They might amass
more samples, to be sure that you're all right.

Because *of course* you are. Even if, right
after she turned twenty, my aunt passed
on, mossy black inside her like a mite-
infested paper-white narcissus, glass-
forced to root in a window's filtered light.
Too many women in this family, mass-

acred by cancer rushing them en masse,
as they stood stunned, slashing left and right,
killing and leaving the rest afraid. Passed
on like a recipe, along with light
blue eyes, fears as strong and old as sea glass.
I want to be like them; I fear I might.

For now, breathe lightly as the forceps pass.
A mass is a mass, no more…Later, write
about the fate that might be held in glass.

Michael T. Young (1968)

My interest in form is an interest in architecture, how a design or structure shapes a space and things move through that structure. Syllable, sound and meter are the raw materials of construction: boards, nails, and cement. Tropes and images are constructed from these, they are the walls, ceiling and floors. Together they shape a mental space. The completed building itself is a poem, which is a kind of thought or idea about the world. These are the habitations we give the mind. Form is the raw material to create these habitations.

I have often considered what I would teach a class of young poets. I always come to the same conclusion: I would teach them form. Form helps a poet control the constituent elements of language: sound and syllable. There is an understanding of these elements that only comes from learning form and it is crucial for poets. Greater control over the constituent elements of language means greater control over language in general and this is equal to a greater power to articulate, a greater ability to penetrate a subject. Form is the basic tool of a poet, like a hammer is the basic tool of a carpenter. No carpenter should be without a hammer. No poet should be without a command of form.

The Fall in Voter Turnout

The pine's elected to the maple's post,
the fly's buzzword is vetoed by the day,
streams in a presidential race all boast
in speeches glittering with icy spray.

The squirrels lobby to protect their nuts,
the honeysuckle prosecutes the bee,
the Sun, pro-lifer that he is, throws fits
about the New Moon's pro-choice policy.

The winds approve this autumn, pass its leaves,
decline more funding to the seed committee.
So every bear believes what he believes,
and all the deer are moving to the city.

Letter from a Baychester Resident

Dear Jack, I'm writing to you from a bus
en route to Pennsylvania. But, of course,
to spare you having to endure this mess
of scribble and these bumps which make it worse,
I'll type it later, with added time to fuss
about deciding to write it out in verse.
Ottava Rima should be long enough—
with bows to Byron — to hold a world in brief.

The road dives into some trees, while the sun
sets down its caldron of gold and brass light
at the clouds' feet. And so it seems, within
these wider spaces, in uncommon flight,
all things are drawn toward their common horizon:
birds, clouds, and poets especially, who write
about the lofty, true and beautiful,
as if their own gravity had no pull.

So, I only aspire to tell you news:
to tell you how things are and how they go,
describe my new apartment, and the muse
that walks the neighborhood, what flowers grow,
the qualities of modest rooms with views,
the picture of wind and weather in the window —
lightning and sudden rain, the kind of frolic
poets impulsively insist symbolic.

The day before the move I cut my finger,
quite severely, on a brandy glass
long used in our Dionysian benders.
Now I bear a mark of that old caprice:
the scar that's forming looks like a forked stinger.
The Doc said, "Keep the hand raise." His advice,
"Make toasts to everyone." And so I try
to praise more, keep my glass full and raised high.

The new apartment's really just a room,
but with enough floor to pace back and forth
which is enough for thought to strut and plume
its feathers, then set off for a warmer North
when the intellect's springtime resumes.
A little room affords the mind great worth,
more than rooms with things of larger cost
where it's easy to lose things and get lost.

A view of brownstones rises from block to block,
receding into water-towers and sky.
New York City's ubiquitous pigeons flock
on building ledges, and like a winged spy,
a gull emerges from clouds, taking stock.
Of what? Not anything we should judge him by,
or judge ourselves, surviving as we do,
feeding the true soul on what isn't true.

Trees and all kinds of flowers line the street:
hibiscus, morning-glories, impatiens, pansies.
Their actual numbers easily defeat
my knowledge of their names. Whatever fancies
the neighbors have, they keep. Discreet,
quiet, they're friendly when I meet their glances,
although the place still has its New York share
of those who talk to you because you're there.

I paid my literary acknowledgment,
strolling by old Wally's, keeping my promise
to memorize "Idea of Order," bent
my step toward the Hotel Chelsea's premises
to see about that balustrade, then went
to the White Horse Tavern, and raised a scotch to Thomas.
And though I haven't bowed to them, Millay
and Cummings didn't live too far away.

There are other things I'd like to tell you,
but they're too poetic for a poem,

such as, "Yeah, and I have a bridge to sell you."
I'll write those out in prose rather than rhyme
hoping to amuse and to compel you,
like these lines, if they've dogged the criticism
of tripping on their feet, being cliché
and leaving me, in closing, yet to say:

The neighborhood is great, and all in all,
things seem to be going well. Though sometimes lonely
and still at work, I feel a gradual
remembrance of myself, of what's my own, free
of expectations which aren't original.
School's started. The poster of Keats you sent me
now hangs above my bed. So I pretend
he helps me dream. Thank you. Write soon.
                              Your friend.

Surfaces

Slow ebbing of the flood tide, gradual
retreat and surrender of the trawler's wake.
As the bottom of the bay rises, a gull
descends and pokes through broken shells and rock.

He scurries furiously back and forth.
He lifts and drops a stone. He tears at clumps
of seaweed, prods a sudden bubbling froth
between his toes, then poses his wings and jumps.

Here, at bottom, there's nothing but survival.
A crab digs deeper in the sand to stay
hidden and undisturbed till the revival
of the moon and the flooding of the bay.

Even the boats betray a need for surface:
their long hulls sunken up to the prow's arc,
their sleek nets dripping, losing significance,
slowly, as they dry all night in the dark.

Notes on the Contributors

Craig Arnold's first book, *Shells*, was the 1998 volume of the Yale Series of Younger Poets. A former Amy Lowell Poetry Traveling Scholar and a Hodder Fellow at Princeton, he has been awarded fellowships from the NEA, Bread Loaf and the MacDowell Colony. His poem "Hot" was selected for the Best American Poetry 1998; others have appeared in *Poetry*, *Paris Review*, *Yale Review*, *The New Republic*, *Gulf Coast* and *Open City*.

Chris Baker earned an MA from the University of Texas at Dallas in 2000. His creative thesis chairman was Fred Turner. Chris's work has appeared in *The Edge City Review*, *The Lyric*, and *Light*. To correspond, please email him at clbakersdozen@yahoo.com.

Bill Coyle was born in Bremerhaven, in what was then West Germany, but grew up in Massachusetts. He currently teaches and tutors at Salem State College in Salem, Massachusetts, and lives with his wife in Boston. His work has appeared in *The Hudson Review*, *The Formalist*, *The Dark Horse*, *Poetry*, and *Literature and Belief*.

Jill Alexander Essbaum won the 1999 Bakeless Prize for her book *Heaven*. She lives and works in Austin, TX where she teaches at Concordia University.

Jenny Factor was born in 1969 in New Haven, CT, and raised in Beverly Hills, CA. She received an A.B. from Harvard and Radcliffe Colleges and an M.F.A. from the Bennington Writing Seminars. Jenny has worked as a contract archaeologist, a Montessori educator, and a writer and editor. She is the recipient of the 2000 Astraea Foundation Grant in Poetry. Her book, *Unraveling at the Name* (Copper Canyon Press, 2002), received the Hayden Carruth Award.

Ted Genoways is the author of *Bullroarer: A Sequence* (Northeastern, 2001), winner of the Samuel French Morse Poetry Prize (selected by Marilyn Hacker), the Natalie Ornish Poetry Award, and the Nebraska Book Award, as well as three chapbooks, most recently *Anna, washing* (Parallel Press, 2001). He is also the editor/translator of *The Selected Poems of Miguel Hernández* (Chicago, 2001), and the editor of several other books, including *Papermill: The Selected Poems* *and Prose Sketches of Joseph Kalar* (Illinois, 2004) and *The Collected Writings of Walt Whitman: The Correspondence, Volume VII* (Iowa, 2004). His awards include a 2003 National Endowment for the Arts Fellowship, a Pushcart Prize, two Guy Owen Poetry Prizes, and the Hackney Literary Award in Poetry.

Beth Gylys is currently an Assistant Professor at Georgia State University. She won the Gerald Cable Poetry First Book Award for her book *Bodies that Hum* (Silverfish Review Press, 1991). She has had work published in many journals including *Paris Review*, *The Southern Review*, *Antioch Review*, *Kenyon Review*, *Ploughshares*, *Boston Review*.

Adam Kirsch is the author of *The Thousand Wells: Poems* (Ivan R. Dee, 2002), which was awarded the New Criterion Poetry Prize. He writes frequently about poetry for *The New Republic*, the *TLS*, and other publications, and is at work on a book about post-World War II American poetry. Born in Los Angeles in 1976, he now lives in New York, where he is the book critic of the *New York Sun*.

April Lindner teaches creative writing at St. Joseph's University in Philadelphia. Her collection, *Skin*, won the 2001 Walt McDonald first book poetry prize, and was published by Texas Tech University Press in spring 2002. She has written two critical monographs—Dana Gioia and New Formalist Poets of the American West—in Boise State University's Western Writer's Series. Her poems have appeared in numerous publications including *The Paris Review*, *Crazyhorse*, *Prairie Schooner*, *Able Muse* (an on-line journal) and *The Formalist*, and have been read by Garrison Keillor on his daily syndicated radio program, The Writer's Almanac, and collected in his anthology *Good Poems*.

Joshua Mehigan edited *Poets & Writers Online* from 1998 to 2001. He now teaches English and freelances as an editor and designer for several poetry-related Web sites. His poems have appeared in *The Formalist*, *Ploughshares*, *Poetry*, *Verse*, and other periodicals. *The Optimist*, his first book of poems, won the Hollis Summers Poetry Prize and will be published in December 2004 by Ohio University Press/Swallow Press.

Joe Osterhaus's first poetry collection, *The Domed Road*, appeared in Take Three: AGNI New Poets Series: 1 (Graywolf Press, 1996). Zoo Press published his second collection, *Radiance*, in 2002. His poems and review articles have appeared in *AGNI*, *The Antioch Review*, *BOMB*, *The Boston Review*, *The Formalist*, *Harvard Review*, *Hotel Amerika*, *The Journal*, *The Nebraska Review*, *The Paris Review*, *Ploughshares*, *Slate*, and *Triquarterly*. His poems also appear in *The New American Poets: A Bread Loaf Anthology* (Middlebury College Press), and *American Poetry: The Next Generation* (Carnegie Mellon Univ. Press). He has taught at Boston University, University College at Washington University, and the Krieger School of Arts and Sciences at Johns Hopkins University. He has master's degrees from Boston University and The University of Chicago.

Alison Pelegrin is author of *The Zydeco Tablets* (Word Press, 2002), as well as two award-winning chapbooks—*Voodoo Lips* (2002) and *Dancing with the One-Armed Man* (1999). For two years she served as Director of the Arkansas Writers in the Schools Program. She lives in Mandeville, Louisiana with her family.

V. Penelope Pelizzon's first book of poems, *Nostos* (Ohio University Press, 2000), was selected for the Hollis Summers Prize and subsequently received the Poetry Society of America's Norma Farber First Book Award. She is working on a new collection for which she received a 2002 Fellowship from the Pennsylvania Council on the Arts. As a critic, Pelizzon has published on literature, photography, and film. With co-author Nancy M. West she has written articles on film noir, including "Reading the Still Photograph in Film Noir" (American Studies, Fall 2002) and "A Perfect Double, Down to the Last Detail" (forthcoming in Postscript). In conjunction with these projects, she is co-authoring a book-length critical study on the relationship between tabloid photography and crime film from the 1920s to the 1960s.

Chelsea Rathburn was born in Jacksonville, Florida, and raised in Miami. She holds degrees from Florida State University and the University of Arkansas. Her poems have appeared in *The New Criterion*, *Sewanee Theological Review*, *The Formalist*, *Pleiades*, *Calyx*, and other journals. Aralia Press published her first chapbook in 2003. She works as a writer and editor for a nonprofit organization in Atlanta.

Jennifer Reeser was born October 30, 1968. Her poems, translations, criticism and fiction have appeared or are forthcoming in U.S., British and Internet journals such as *Louisiana Literature*, *Disquieting Muses*, *Pivot*, *Blue Unicorn*,

The New Laurel Review, and *Able Muse*. Her work has been nominated for a Pushcart and her collection, *An Alabaster Flask*, is the winner of the Word Press First Book Prize, was published in 2003. *Winterproof*, her second collection, will be published by Word Press in 2005. She lives in Louisiana with her husband Jason and their five children.

A. E. Stallings' first collection, *Archaic Smile*, received the 1999 Richard Wilbur Award. Her work has twice been included in the Best American Poetry series (1994, 2000), has received a Pushcart prize and other awards, and appears widely in US journals. She is completing a verse translation of Lucretius' *De Rerum Natura* for Penguin Classics. Stallings lives in Athens, Greece, with her husband, John Psaropoulos, the editor of *The Athens News*.

Philip Stephens is the author of *The Determined Days*, a poetry collection, and a chapbook, *The Signalmen*.

Diane Thiel is the author of *Echolocations* (2000), which received the Nicholas Roerich Prize from Story Line Press and Writing Your Rhythm (2001), as well as an Aralia chapbook, *Cleft in the Wall* (1999). Her work appears in *Poetry*, *The Hudson Review*, and *Best American Poetry 1999* and is re-printed in Longman, Bedford, Harper Collins, Henry Holt and McGraw Hill anthologies. She received her BA and MFA from Brown University. Thiel was a Fulbright Scholar for 2001-2002 and is currently an Assistant Professor at the University of New Mexico. (www.dianethiel.net)

Jennifer Tonge holds an M.F.A. from the University of Utah. Her awards include a Wisconsin Institute for Creative Writing fellowship, scholarships from the Bread Loaf Writers' Conference, and fellowships from The MacDowell Colony, The Virginia Center for the Creative Arts, The Ucross Foundation, and The Djerassi Resident Artists Program.

Catherine Tufariello was born in Ithaca, N.Y. in 1963 and raised upstate, near Buffalo. She studied literature at SUNY Buffalo and at Cornell University, where she received a Ph.D. in 1994. Since then she has taught at colleges and universities in New York, South Carolina, and Florida. She has published two chapbooks of poetry, *Free Time* (R.L. Barth, 2001) and *Annunciations* (Aralia Press, 2001). Her poems have appeared in numerous periodicals and anthologies, including *Poetry*, *The Hudson Review*, *The Poetry Anthology: 1912-2002*, *The New Penguin Book of Love Poetry*, and the *Longman* literature anthology edited by R. S. Gwynn. Her first full-length collection, titled *Keeping My Name*, won the Walt McDonald First Book Competition and was published by Texas Tech University Press. She lives in Brooklyn with her husband and daughter.

Kevin Walzer holds a Ph.D. in English from the University in Cincinnati. His poetry collections include *Living in Cincinnati* (1995) and *Greater Circles* (2001). His critical book, *The Ghost of Tradition: Expansive Poetry and Postmodernism* (1998), was named an Outstanding Book by Choice.

Rachel Wetzsteon was born in New York City in 1967, and received a B.A. in English from Yale, an M.A. from the Johns Hopkins Writing Seminars, and a Ph.D. in English from Columbia. Her first book of poems, *The Other Stars*, was selected for the 1993 National Poetry Series and published by Penguin in 1994; her second book, *Home and Away*, was published by Penguin in 1998. She received the 2001 Witter Bynner Prize for Poetry from the American Academy of Arts and Letters, and currently teaches at William Paterson University.

Sonny Williams was raised in Dallas, Texas and received his B.A. from the University of North Texas and studied for his doctorate at the University of Texas at Dallas. He has edited another anthology, *Story Hour: Contemporary Narratives by American Poets*. Currently, he teaches at the University of New Orleans.

Greg Williamson's first book, *The Silent Partner*, won the Nicholas Roerich Poetry Prize from Story Line Press in 1995. *Errors in the Script*, published by Overlook Press, was a runner-up for the 2003 Poet's Prize.

Christian Wiman was born and raised in west Texas and holds a B.A. in English Literature from Washington and Lee University. He has taught at Northwestern, Stanford, Lynchburg College in Virginia, and the Prague School of Economics. His first book, *The Long Home*, won the 1998 Nicholas Roerich Prize and was published by Story Line Press. His second book, *Hard Night*, is forthcoming from Copper Canyon Press in 2005. His poems, criticism, and personal essays appear widely in such magazines as *The Atlantic Monthly*, *Harper's*, *The Threepenny Review*, *Slate*, *Poetry*, and elsewhere. He has won the Ruth Lilly Fellowship from the Modern Poetry Association, a Wallace Stegner Fellowship from Stanford University, a Dobie-Paisano Fellowship from the University of Texas-Austin, a Pushcart Prize, and a Gerald Freund Grant from the Whiting

Foundation. He lives in Chicago and is editor of *Poetry*.

Chryss Yost has published two chapbooks, *La Jolla Boys* (Mille Grazie, 2000) and *Escaping from Autopia* (Oberon, 1998). She runs a poetry series in Santa Barbara and is a book columnist for the *Santa Barbara Independent*. She is the co-editor of two poetry anthologies: *California Poetry* (with Dana Gioia) and *Poetry Daily Unplugged* (with Diane Boller and Don Selby). She is also an editor of *Solo*, a literary journal. Her poetry has been widely published and anthologized. She lives with her daughter, Cassidy, three dogs, and a tortoise.

Michael T. Young has published in numerous journals including *Blue Unicorn*, *The Christian Science Monitor*, *Folio*, *The Hollins Critic*, and *Pivot*. His first full-length collection, *Transcriptions of Daylight*, was published by Rattapallax Press in September 2000. He was nominated for a 2001 Pushcart Prize. His chapbook, *Because the Wind Has Questions*, was published by Somers Rocks Press in 1997. He was a semi-finalist for the 1992 Discovery/The Nation Contest and received honorable mention for the 1997 Catalina Páez & Seumas MacManus Award given by Hunter College and sponsored by the Academy of American Poets.

About the Editor

Sonny Williams was raised in Dallas, Texas and received his B.A. from the University of North Texas and studied for his doctorate at the University of Texas at Dallas. He has edited another anthology, *Story Hour: Contemporary Narratives by American Poets*, published by Story Line Press. Currently, he teaches at the University of New Orleans.

About the Artist

David Bates was born in Dallas, Texas and continues to live there. He studied at Southern Methodist University where he received a BFA in 1975 and an MFA in 1978. In 1976 he attended the Independent Study program at the Whitney Museum of Art in New York. In 1987 his work was included in the prestigious Whitney Museum of American Art Biennial. His work is represented in the collections of the Whitney Museum of Art, the Metropolitan Museum of Art, the National Museum of Art, and the Hirshhorn Museum and Sculpture Garden in Washington, the Carnegie Museum of Art in Pittsburgh, the Modern Art Museum of Fort Worth and the Dallas Museum of Fine Arts.

David Bates conveys an authentic, deeply felt sense of place in his work. He paints and draws in his Dallas studio but goes to Walla Walla, Washington to make his sculpture. Much of his work has been influenced by folk art and outside art, genres that he feels close to, that are natural to him even if he is not a self-taught artist and his subjects' lives are not his. He is not, though, trying to be a folk artist. He dismisses the notion of regionalism as art of a lesser order. "I can't lean any other way. This is where I live."

Printed in the United States
23929LVS00005B/269